Motion Junction	 Strong Museum of Play	 Kids Canyon	 Karpus Family Playground
 Seneca Lake State Park	 Sweden Town Park	 First Responder's Park	 Adventure Towers
 Warsaw Village Park	 Letchworth State Park	 Sampson State Park	 Pineway Ponds Park
 Basil Marella Park	Sodus Point Beach Park	 Egypt Park	 Kreag Road Park
 Jack's Place, Webster Park	 Al Lorenz Park	 Cayuga Lake State Park	 Irondequoit Bay Marine Park

Rochester's Playbook

100 Loved Playgrounds Around Rochester NY

2024

Copyright © 2023 Sara Snyder
All rights reserved

No portion of this book may be reproduced in any form without permission from the publisher, except as permitted by U.S. copyright law. For permissions contact: ssnyder@rochesterplaybook.com

ISBN: 979-8-9894705-0-1

Rochester's Playbook: 100 Loved Playgrounds Around Rochester NY
Author: Sara Snyder
Photography: Sara Snyder, Kiley Hanje, Michelle Weimer, Jocelyn Semple, Lauren Bacher, Nicolette Reidy
Map design: Forest Swaciak

A special thank you to Kiley Hanje, Michelle Weimer, Jenn Beideman and Bethany Ball for editing and feedback.

Printed in USA

First Edition: November 2023

www.rochesterplaybook.com

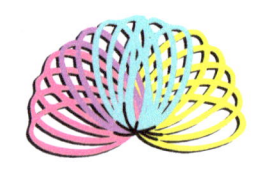

for Isaac and Julia

LET'S *get* PLAYING!

This book is jam packed with our favorite playgrounds around the Greater Rochester area! Before you get exploring, here are a couple of notes:

EACH PAGE WILL HAVE 3 KEYS:

The key at the top is for bathrooms:

- Bathroom shelter*
- Outhouse*
- No Bathrooms**

The second key indicates whether the playground is fenced in or not:

- The playground is entirely fenced in with at least one latching gate and no openings.
- The playground is mostly fenced in but lacks a gate. There may be a large gap in the fence at the entrance.
- The playground is either not fenced in or the fence does not encompass the majority of the playground.

The third key indicates whether the 'Extend the trip' activity is within walking distance or not:

- The activity is within the park or very close with sidewalks.
- It is best to drive to the activity.
- You can either take a stroll or make a short drive to the activity.

*Bathroom shelters and outhouses are often not available in the fall - early spring

**If bathrooms are not available at a park, there is likely an establishment nearby with public restrooms

How are the playgrounds organized in the book?

To make playground hopping a cinch, the playgrounds are listed by location! The table of contents on the following page and the map that follows list all the playgrounds in the book alongside their page numbers.

How are playgrounds chosen for this book?

We make every effort to discover all the public playgrounds in Greater Rochester, including parks in Monroe, Genesee, Livingston, Ontario, Orleans, Seneca, Wayne, Wyoming, and Yates Counties. We do not include school playgrounds, member-only access playgrounds, or playgrounds that are only available for a short season. Our aim is to feature only playgrounds that are accessible year-round, at any time of the day.

Each visited playground is scored on a scale of 1-10 in the following categories:

- **Condition:** Is the park well-maintained? Is there graffiti and/or garbage? Are the playground structures old or new?
- **Uniqueness:** Is there a 'wow-factor'? Are the structures common or unusual?
- **Surrounding environment:** Are there other activities in the area? Is the park picturesque and inviting?
- **Popularity:** Is the playground well-loved by the community?
- **Playability:** Does the playground captivate kids and spark imagination? How long does the park hold their attention?
- **Accessibility:** Does the playground accommodate wheelchairs? Is the equipment reachable by stroller? This will be noted under 'Wheel Friendly Features' on each playground page.
- **Inclusivity:** Does the playground consider kids of various age groups and abilities, sensory needs, financial backgrounds, transportation capabilities, etc.
- **Amenities:** Are there bathrooms, picnic tables, grills benches, etc?

Selecting the playgrounds for this book was a challenging task. Rochester boasts numerous beautiful parks, so we carefully evaluated each playground based on the criteria mentioned earlier. Please note that some parks have multiple playgrounds. In most cases, we did not dedicate a separate page to each playground to make room for others. You can find information about additional playgrounds within the park in the 'Extend the Trip' activity section.

Every playground included in the book was visited and assessed in 2023. However, we acknowledge that playground conditions can change rapidly. If you come across any such changes or know of a playground that should be considered for inclusion in the book, please let us know at update@rochesterplaybook.com.

Why do we love playgrounds so much?

So glad you asked! Playgrounds hold a special place in our communities, as they are more than just places for children to play. These spaces bring together families from all walks of life, providing a shared setting where children of different backgrounds, abilities, and ages can strengthen their physical and social skills. Parents also benefit by bonding with one another, forming a network of support and shared experiences. Playgrounds get kids moving outside, fostering a love for the outdoors and active lifestyles. Numerous studies have shown that play is a critical piece in child development, promoting cognitive, emotional, and physical growth. Therefore, playgrounds are hubs of discovery, where children learn and grow through exploration, creativity, and interaction. The memories formed in these dynamic settings become the foundation of a community, fostering connections, understanding, and inclusivity that enrich our lives. In essence, playgrounds are where the tapestry of our society is woven, one joyful moment and shared adventure at a time.

100 PLAYGROUNDS
TABLE OF CONTENTS
(AND CHECKLIST!)

- [ ] 1. Strong Museum of Play
- [ ] 2. Genesee Gateway Park
- [ ] 3. Bronson Avenue Playground
- [ ] 4. Ellwanger and Barry Park
- [ ] 5. Lilac Adventure Zone
- [ ] 6. Merriman Park Playground
- [ ] 7. Grand Avenue Playground
- [ ] 8. Cobbs Hill Park
- [ ] 9. Genesee Valley Park
- [ ] 10. Campbell Street R-Center
- [ ] 11. Brighton Town Hall
- [ ] 12. Buckland Park
- [ ] 13. Meridian Centre Park
- [ ] 14. Lions Park
- [ ] 15. Kids Canyon Playground
- [ ] 16. Goodwin Park
- [ ] 17. Veterans Park, Greece
- [ ] 18. Basil Marella Park
- [ ] 19. Columbus Park
- [ ] 20. Seneca Park
- [ ] 21. Camp Eastman
- [ ] 22. Durand Eastman Park
- [ ] 23. Heyer-Bayer Memorial Park
- [ ] 24. Irondequoit Bay Marine Park
- [ ] 25. Sandbar Park
- [ ] 26. Webster Park
- [ ] 27. Kent Park
- [ ] 28. First Responders Park
- [ ] 29. Karpus Family Playground
- [ ] 30. Abraham Lincoln Park
- [ ] 31. Rothfuss Park
- [ ] 32. Veterans Park, Penfield
- [ ] 33. Edmund Lyon Park
- [ ] 34. Perinton Park
- [ ] 35. Fellows Road Park
- [ ] 36. Center Park West
- [ ] 37. Egypt Park
- [ ] 38. Kreag Road Park
- [ ] 39. Powder Mills Park
- [ ] 40. Thornell Farm Park
- [ ] 41. Great Embankment Park
- [ ] 42. Pittsford Community Center
- [ ] 43. Veterans Park, Henrietta
- [ ] 44. Mendon Ponds Park
- [ ] 45. Dreisbach Splash Park
- [ ] 46. Harry Allen Park
- [ ] 47. Town of Rush Playground
- [ ] 48. Breese Park
- [ ] 49. Black Creek Park
- [ ] 50. Union Station Park

- [ ] 51. Ogden Town Offices Park
- [ ] 52. Pineway Ponds Park
- [ ] 53. Adventure Towers Playground
- [ ] 54. Alpine Adventure Zone
- [ ] 55. Clarkson Recreation Park
- [ ] 56. Barry Street Park
- [ ] 57. Sweden Town Park
- [ ] 58. Hamlin Recreation Center
- [ ] 59. Partyka Farms
- [ ] 60. Hamlin Beach State Park
- [ ] 61. Yates Park
- [ ] 62. Bullard Park
- [ ] 63. Pine Street Park
- [ ] 64. Genesee County Park
- [ ] 65. Attica Memorial Park
- [ ] 66. Warsaw Village Park
- [ ] 67. Perry Village Park
- [ ] 68. Letchworth, Lower Falls
- [ ] 69. Letchworth, Wolf Creek
- [ ] 70. Letchworth, Highbanks Area
- [ ] 71. Mount Morris Dam
- [ ] 72. Al Lorenz Park
- [ ] 73. Avon Driving Park
- [ ] 74. Mark Tubbs Park
- [ ] 75. Sandy Bottom Park
- [ ] 76. RMSC Cumming Nature Center
- [ ] 77. Ontario County Park
- [ ] 78. Onanda Park
- [ ] 79. Kershaw Park
- [ ] 80. Frank Baker Park
- [ ] 81. Richard P. Outhouse Park
- [ ] 82. Motion Junction Playground
- [ ] 83. Dryer Road Park
- [ ] 84. Victor Municipal Park
- [ ] 85. Mertensia Park
- [ ] 86. Farmington Town Park
- [ ] 87. Ginegaw Park
- [ ] 88. Marion Town Park
- [ ] 89. Casey Park
- [ ] 90. B. Foreman Park
- [ ] 91. Sodus Point Beach Park
- [ ] 92. John Brown Memorial Park
- [ ] 93. Phelps Community Center
- [ ] 94. Red Jacket Park
- [ ] 95. Geneva Community Lakefront Park
- [ ] 96. Finger Lakes Welcome Center
- [ ] 97. Seneca Lake State Park
- [ ] 98. Sampson State Park
- [ ] 99. Lodi Point State Marine Park
- [ ] 100. Cayuga Lake State Park

Orleans

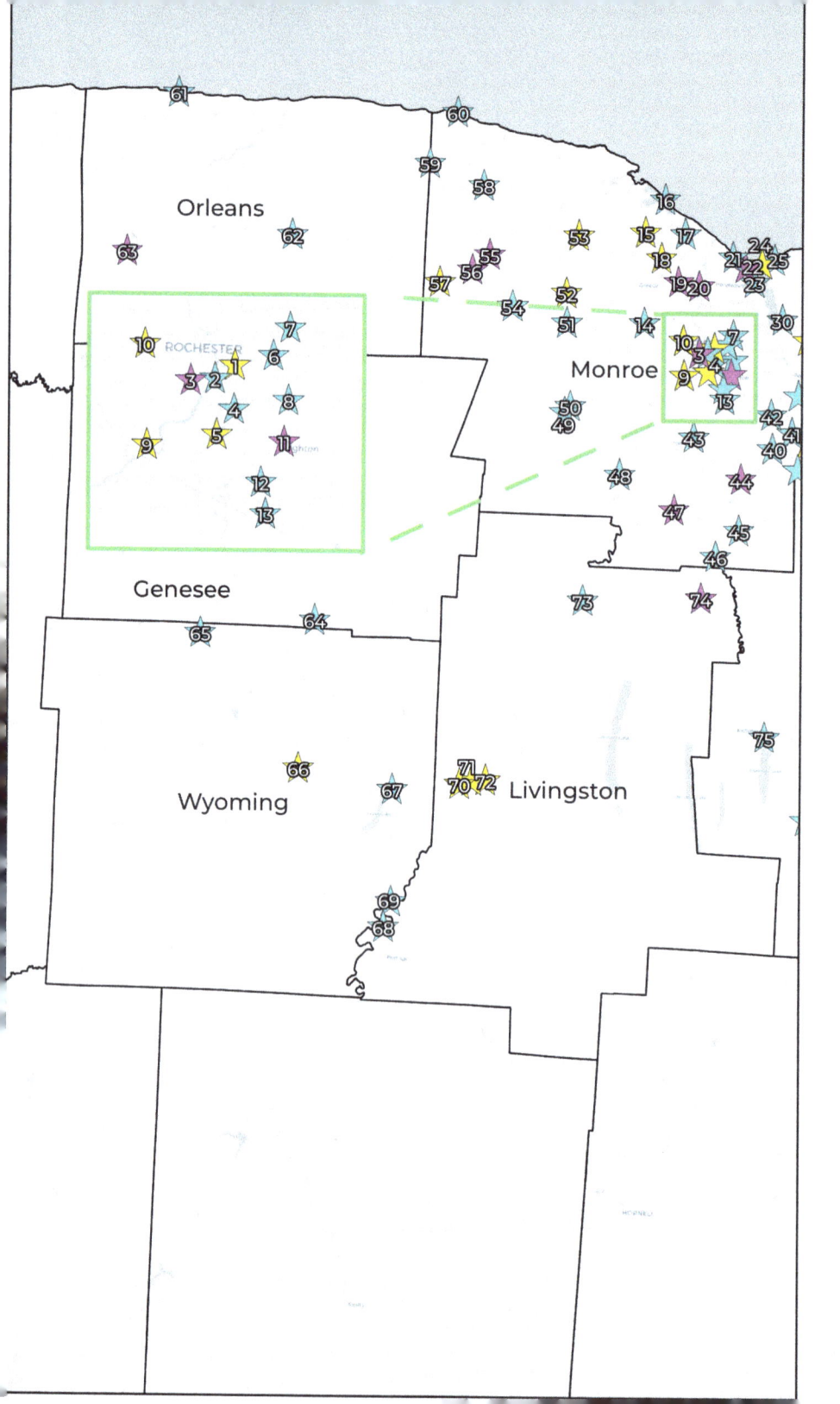

Monroe

Genesee

Wyoming Livingston

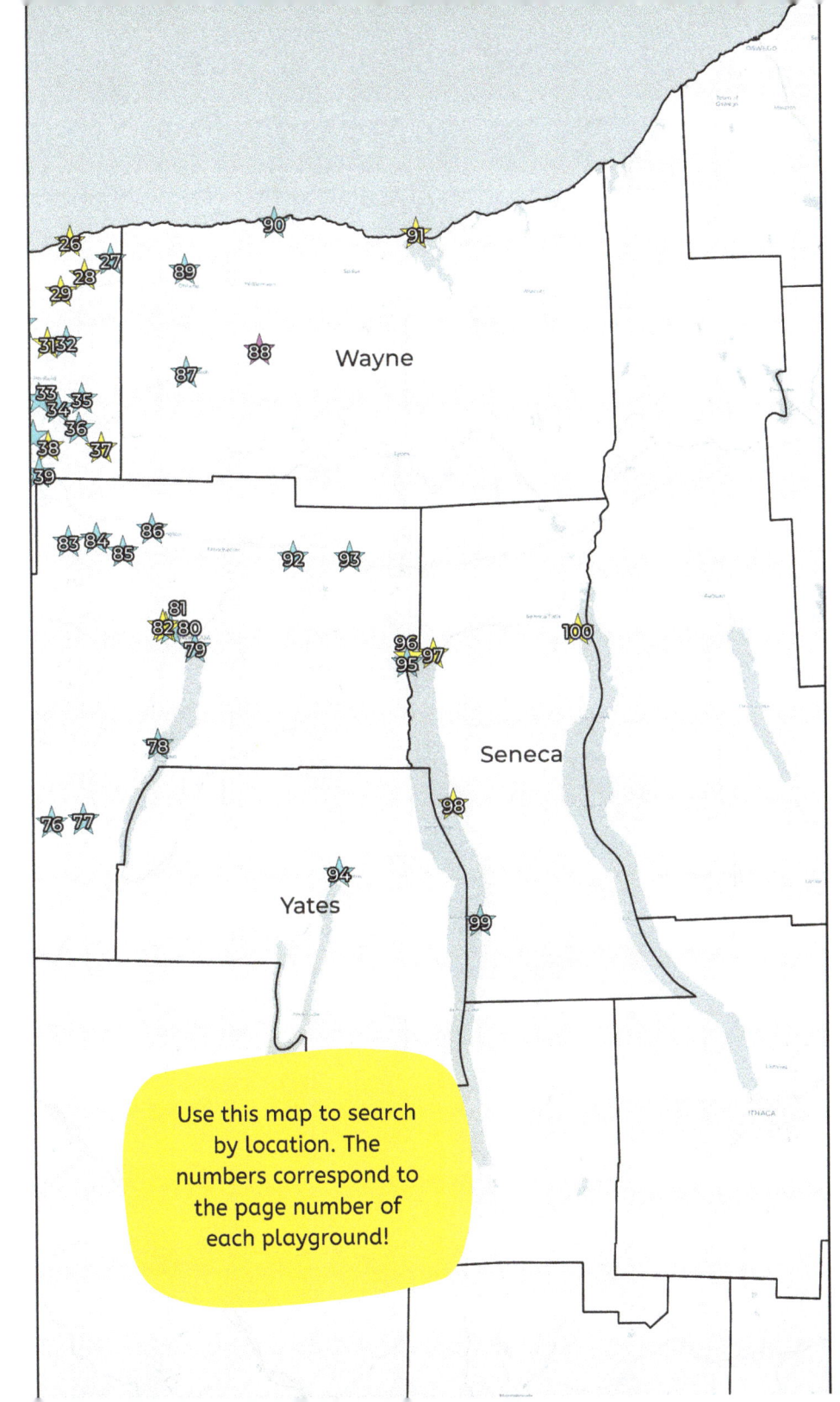

Use this map to search by location. The numbers correspond to the page number of each playground!

1 MANHATTAN SQUARE DR, ROCHESTER, NY 14607

STRONG MUSEUM OF PLAY

PLAYGROUND DETAILS

Condition: Excellent condition, new and well maintained

Surface: Turf and cement

Shade: The play area is in direct sun, there is a small overhang outside as well as the the air conditioned museum steps away

Sand Play: No

Water Play: No

Picnic: Cafe and cafeteria inside museum

Creeks/Lakes: None

Wheel Friendly Features: Museum and outdoor play space is wheel friendly, includes accessible we-go-round in outdoor play area

Cost: Admission to museum required to enter outdoor play area

SWINGS
Regular: 0
Adaptive: 0
Baby: 0
Tire: 0
Tandem: 0

SUMMARY

The new outdoor area at the Museum of Play encourages guests to engage in active play as they explore a landscape inspired by classic board games. There's a game of "Simon" that works well as a cooperative experience with family and friends. Kids can also take a spin on the Game of Life "spinner" and move that many spaces down the Candy Land path.

EXTEND THE TRIP

The outdoor play area is just a small part of what the Strong Museum has to offer. Inside, you can explore the Play Lab, Toy Hall of Fame, Wegmans Super Kids Market, Reading Adventureland, Pinball Playfields (remember to bring cash for tokens), Imagination Destination, and much more! Snacks, beverages, and packed lunches are permitted and can be enjoyed in the cafeteria, or you can purchase food at one of the many dining options within the museum.

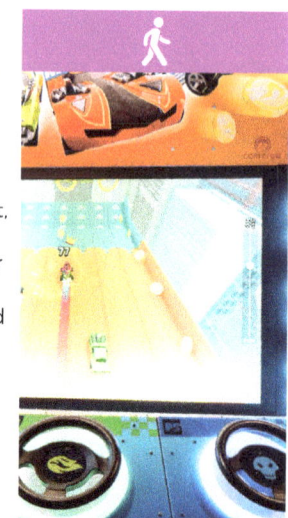

Strong Museum Interior

151 MT HOPE AVE, ROCHESTER, NY 14620

GENESEE GATEWAY PARK

SUMMARY

Genesee Gateway Park earns a perfect 10/10 for its 'wow factor'! This playground beautifully complements the surrounding landscape and adds a unique, fun dimension to our city. Although it's on the smaller side, there are play structures here for all ages. A word of caution: the metal slide is quite fast and is especially enjoyed by older kids.

PLAYGROUND DETAILS

Condition: The playground is new, however, not always maintained

Surface: Rubber

Shade: None

Sand Play: No

Water Play: No

Picnic: Large rocks for sitting and several grills, no picnic tables or pavilions

Creeks/Lakes: The Genesee River is a short walk from the playground, keep a close eye!

Wheel Friendly Features: Zero grade entry to rubber surface

Cost: Free

SWINGS
Regular: 0
Adaptive: 0
Baby: 0
Tire: 0
Tandem: 0

EXTEND THE TRIP

Central Library is just a 2-minute drive from the playground! The Children's section of Central Library is situated in the Bausch & Lomb Library Building, right next to the Court Street Parking Garage. It's located on the second floor and can be accessed by stairs or elevator. From the hidden room to the playhouse and cars, there are plenty of opportunities for play here!

Central Library of Rochester
115 South Ave, Rochester, NY 14604

15 CADY ST, ROCHESTER, NY 14608
BRONSON AVENUE PLAYGROUND

PLAYGROUND DETAILS

Condition: Excellent, built in 2022

Surface: Rubber

Shade: None

Sand Play: No

Water Play: No

Picnic: There's an "outdoor classroom" consisting of large rocks to sit on

Creeks/Lakes: None

Wheel Friendly Features: Zero grade entry to rubber surface

Cost: Free

SWINGS
Regular: 0
Adaptive: 0
Baby: 0
Tire: 0
Tandem: 0

SUMMARY

Bronson Avenue Playground boasts two distinct play structures, an inviting rock wall apparatus, a unique bridge, musical instruments, and an 'outdoor classroom' area. It's an excellent place to visit when you're at the Phillis Wheatley Community Library. While there isn't a restroom at the playground, you can access a public restroom within the library during its open hours.

EXTEND THE TRIP

The Phillis Wheatley Community Library is right across the street from Bronson Avenue Playground. The children's section of the library offers a variety of books to explore, along with a play kitchen, puzzles, computers, dolls, and more!

Phillis Wheatley Community Library
33 Dr Samuel McCree Way, Rochester, NY 14608

3

890 MEIGS ST, ROCHESTER, NY 14620

ELLWANGER & BARRY PARK

SUMMARY

Ellwanger and Barry Park features a rubber play surface in some areas, a large sandbox, community-donated toys, and a modern play structure for older kids. For the younger kids, there's a miniature clubhouse and slide. It's important to note that there is limited street parking, the playground is situated close to the road with limited fencing, and there are no on-site restrooms.

EXTEND THE TRIP

Take a walk or a quick drive down Meigs Street to The Playhouse/Swillburger. Here, you'll discover made-to-order burgers, fries, shakes, and a variety of dietary options, including vegan, dairy-free, and gluten-free choices. The venue is filled with arcade games, featuring 30 classic favorites like Mario Kart, Tetris, and Skeeball. It's a great spot for a fun lunch after your time at the playground!

The Playhouse/Swillburger.
820 S Clinton Ave, Rochester, NY 14620

PLAYGROUND DETAILS

Condition: Playground is in great shape: built in 2019, some of the toys may be broken

Surface: Mostly rubber

Shade: Shaded green space surrounding playground

Sand Play: Yes

Water Play: No

Picnic: Limited picnic tables, shaded lawn for picnic blanket

Creeks/Lakes: None

Wheel Friendly Features: Zero grade entry to rubber surface and wide paved path in some areas of park

Cost: Free

SWINGS
Regular: 2
Adaptive: 0
Baby: 2
Tire: 0
Tandem: 0

249 HIGHLAND AVE, ROCHESTER, NY 14620

LILAC ADVENTURE ZONE

PLAYGROUND DETAILS

Condition: Built in 2018 and showing some wear

Surface: Mulch

Shade: Limited shaded green space surrounding playground as well as small picnic shelters

Sand Play: No

Water Play: No

Picnic: Limited picnic tables, shaded lawn for picnic blanket

Creeks/Lakes: None

Wheel Friendly Features: None at playground, accessible lilac grove nearby

Cost: Free

SWINGS
Regular: 0
Adaptive: 0
Baby: 0
Tire: 0
Tandem: 0

SUMMARY

This playground within Highland Park is unique for its use of logs as the primary material for its structures. Consequently, you'll encounter mainly steps, bridges, and balance beams, making it more suitable for older kids. It's highly recommended to wear sneakers when visiting this playground!

EXTEND THE TRIP

Lamberton Conservatory is a 5-10 minute walk or a 2-minute drive away. It's a fantastic year-round destination, providing warmth and beauty in the midst of winter and making for a great stop for those enjoying the playground and hiking the trails in the summer. Children adore the wide variety of plant life and the chance to observe quails and turtles as they roam around the conservatory grounds. Visiting the Conservatory is very affordable, with day passes priced at only a few dollars and memberships also available.

Lamberton Conservatory
180 Reservoir Ave, Rochester, NY 14620

MERRIMAN ST, ROCHESTER, NY 14607

MERRIMAN PARK PLAYGROUND

SUMMARY

At Merriman Street Playground off University Avenue, you'll discover two new play structures. The first structure is designed for kids aged 5 to 12 and includes exciting climbing elements and a tall slide. The second structure is perfect for toddlers, featuring a small slide and low-level climbing features.

EXTEND THE TRIP

You can explore the Neighborhood of the Arts along the art trail, starting from the playground and heading towards the Memorial Art Gallery (MAG). If you prefer, you can skip the walk, park at the MAG and explore the art on the grounds there. Kids will have fun climbing stairs, walking through the tree-covered path, and interacting with the sculptures.

Memorial Art Gallery Grounds
500 University Ave, Rochester, NY 14607

PLAYGROUND DETAILS

Condition: New, built in 2021

Surface: Rubber

Shade: None

Sand Play: No

Water Play: No

Picnic: There's a single picnic table and some green space, alternatively, you can stroll down University Avenue for cafe options

Creeks/Lakes: None

Wheel Friendly Features: Zero grade entry to rubber surface, stroll from playground to MAG is wheel friendly

Cost: Free

SWINGS
Regular: 0
Adaptive: 0
Baby: 0
Tire: 0
Tandem: 0

250 GRAND AVE, ROCHESTER, NY 14609

GRAND AVENUE PARK

PLAYGROUND DETAILS

Condition: Good, with some wear

Surface: Rubber

Shade: Minimal shade from trees

Sand Play: No

Water Play: No

Picnic: Several benches, limited picnic tables

Creeks/Lakes: None

Wheel Friendly Features: Zero grade entry to rubber surface

Cost: Free

SWINGS
Regular: 2
Adaptive: 0
Baby: 2
Tire: 0
Tandem: 0

SUMMARY

Grand Avenue Park playground offers both a typical playground and a Ninja Course designed for ages 13+. Here, you'll find something for all ages, including regular swings and baby swings, interactive and sensory features, climbing structures, an open grassy area, and more!

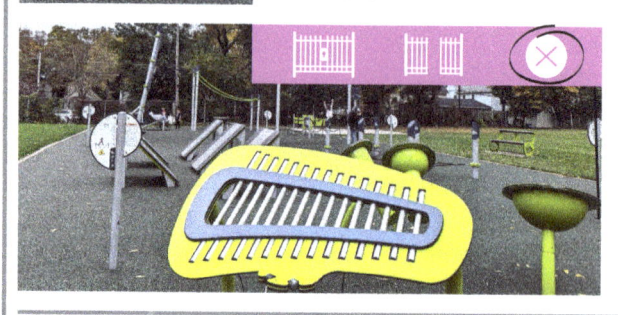

EXTEND THE TRIP

Walk or drive to New City Cafe & Roastery for delicious coffee and a treat before or after your playground visit. The cafe offers a great selection, friendly staff, a cozy atmosphere, and fair prices!

New City Cafe & Roastery
441 Parsells Ave, Rochester, NY 14609

100 NORRIS DR, ROCHESTER, NY 14610
COBBS HILL PARK

SUMMARY
The playground located in Cobbs Hills Park is unique due to its inclusion of a parkour-style obstacle course. This course is equipped with a challenge board that outlines the path of the course. The playground can be found on Norris Drive, directly across from Lake Riley Lodge. A smaller playground is right nearby.

PLAYGROUND DETAILS

Condition: The parkour course is well loved and in need of some repair

Surface: Turf

Shade: Shaded green space surrounding playground

Sand Play: No

Water Play: No

Picnic: Picnic tables and grills throughout park

Creeks/Lakes: Lake across the street from playground

Wheel Friendly Features: None

Cost: Free

SWINGS
Regular: 0
Adaptive: 0
Baby: 0
Tire: 0
Tandem: 0

EXTEND THE TRIP
If you're up for a challenge, hike up to the reservoir from the playground. Start by heading toward Monroe Ave and the Tennis courts. You'll eventually find a gravel path leading around the tennis courts and up the hill to the reservoir. The hike is just under 0.5 miles and follows a there-and-back trail. Additionally, there's a 0.69-mile paved track around the reservoir. Please be cautious when climbing the stairs with kids, as there's a road between the stairs and the reservoir.

Cobbs Hill Reservoir
Reservoir Rd, Rochester, NY 14610

1316 GENESEE ST, ROCHESTER NY 14611
GENESEE VALLEY PARK PLAYGROUND FOR ALL CHILDREN

PLAYGROUND DETAILS

Condition: Good, with some wear

Surface: Rubber

Shade: Shaded green space surrounding playground

Sand Play: No

Water Play: Public pool a short walk or drive away

Picnic: Limited picnic tables

Creeks/Lakes: The Genesee River winds throughout the park, but not close to this playground

Wheel Friendly Features: Zero grade entry to rubber surface and bathrooms, paved paths throughout park

Cost: Free

SWINGS
Regular: 4
Adaptive: 0
Baby: 2
Tire: 0
Tandem: 1

SUMMARY

This playground features a variety of inclusive structures and apparatuses designed for a wide range of ages and abilities. The 'ropes course' is particularly appealing to older children, while various slides and spinning mechanisms cater to others.

EXTEND THE TRIP

The Genesee Valley Sports Complex features an outdoor pool that's about a 5-minute walk or a 2-minute drive from the playground. A small fee is required for pool use. Check online for costs and the open swim schedule:
www.cityofrochester.gov/GVPSC/

Alternatively, there are several stroller-friendly trails and pedestrian bridges throughout Genesee Valley Park to explore.

Genesee Valley Park Pedestrian Bridge

524 CAMPBELL ST, ROCHESTER, NY 14611

CAMPBELL STREET R-CENTER

SUMMARY

The playground at Campbell Street R-Center is situated right behind the splash pad, well away from the road. There are two sections to this playground: one for older kids and one for younger ones. The 5-12 playground features a 'repelling wall,' a spiral slide, monkey bars, and more. The splash pad is just steps away, perfect for cooling off! Bathrooms are available within the R-Center when it's open.

PLAYGROUND DETAILS

Condition: Built in 2018, in good shape and well maintained

Surface: Rubber (playground), cement (splash pad)

Shade: No

Sand Play: No

Water Play: Splash pad

Picnic: Limited picnic tables

Creeks/Lakes: None

Wheel Friendly Features: Zero grade entry to rubber surface, splash pad is fully accessible

Cost: Free

SWINGS
Regular: 0
Adaptive: 0
Baby: 0
Tire: 0
Tandem: 0

EXTEND THE TRIP

Before heading out, consider reserving a spot for an informative tour through Susan B. Anthony's home. The tour takes about 45 minutes and costs $15 for adults, with discounts for seniors, students, and military members. Inside the house, you'll find many of Susan B. Anthony's personal belongings. Don't forget to visit the small gift shop next door! The Susan B. Anthony Museum and House is just a 4-minute drive from the playground. Additionally, Susan B. Anthony Square Park is a 1-minute drive or a 3-minute walk from the House/Museum.

Susan B. Anthony Square Park
39 King St, Rochester, NY 14608

10

2300 ELMWOOD AVE, ROCHESTER, NY 14618
BRIGHTON TOWN HALL PLAYGROUND

PLAYGROUND DETAILS

Condition: Fair

Surface: Mulch

Shade: Baby swings in shade, the rest of the playground is in direct sun

Sand Play: No

Water Play: The town pool is located directly behind the playground and is open to the public for a small entry fee (the pool is fenced in)

Picnic: Some benches at playground, pavilion with picnic tables behind pool

Creeks/Lakes: None

Wheel Friendly Features: Paved path leads to rocking boat apparatus and continues on through nearby neighborhood

Cost: Free

SWINGS
Regular: 2
Adaptive: 0
Baby: 2
Tire: 0
Tandem: 0

SUMMARY

While this playground is in need of updates, it's cherished by the community for its proximity to the library and public pool. There's ample green space nearby for picnics and play. However, the playground is close to the parking lot, so keep a close eye on children. A path from the playground leads to a peaceful neighborhood for strolling or biking. Restrooms are available in the nearby library during its open hours.

EXTEND THE TRIP

The Brighton Library is just steps away from the playground and offers an entire room dedicated to play. This indoor playroom features a craft station, baby dolls, a kitchen, and more. The room is often filled with kids, so your little one will likely find a playmate there. You can find the playroom in the rear of the children's section of the library.

Brighton Library
2300 Elmwood Ave, Rochester, NY 14618

1341 WESTFALL RD, ROCHESTER, NY 14618

BUCKLAND PARK

SUMMARY

Featured here is the first playground at Buckland Park, but there are two others in the park! This initial playground features the beloved car play structure, tunnel slides, climbing slides, and a climbing wall. It's the only playground in the park with a covered pavilion and picnic tables nearby.

EXTEND THE TRIP

Bring bikes, scooters, a stroller, or a wagon to explore the rest of the park! It's a great space for playground hopping without needing to return to your car. Alternatively, the open fields provide an excellent opportunity for flying a kite. If you walk a bit further, you can have an educational experience at the Historic Buckland Farmhouse (by appointment only) and visit the community garden.

Buckland Park playground #3

PLAYGROUND DETAILS

Condition: Good

Surface: Mulch

Shade: Playground in direct sun, some trees and pavilions for shade

Sand Play: No

Water Play: No

Picnic: Several picnic tables and plenty of space for a picnic blanket throughout park

Creeks/Lakes: None

Wheel Friendly Features: Wide paved paths throughout park

Cost: Free

SWINGS
Regular: 2
Adaptive: 0
Baby: 2
Tire: 0
Tandem: 0

2025 MERIDIAN CENTRE BLVD, ROCHESTER, NY 14618

MERIDIAN CENTRE PARK

PLAYGROUND DETAILS

Condition: Excellent

Surface: Mulch

Shade: None

Sand Play: No

Water Play: No

Picnic: Several picnic tables nearby

Creeks/Lakes: Erie Canal a short stroll away

Wheel Friendly Features: Wide paved paths throughout park

Cost: Free

SWINGS
Regular: 2
Adaptive: 0
Baby: 2
Tire: 0
Tandem: 0

SUMMARY

Meridian Centre Park is a hidden gem just off the 590! Don't be deceived by the business complex at the front; there are hiking trails, canal paths, and open fields to explore. The playground can be a bit challenging to find, as it's tucked behind the business park. Drive to the rear of the complex and park in the back of the parking lot off Summit Circle Drive.

EXTEND THE TRIP

Behind the playground, you'll find paved paths for practicing bike riding or pushing a stroller. There's also a butterfly garden nearby, and the Erie Canal Heritage Trail is just a short walk away. To access the Canal Path quickly, head south down the path from the playground (this trail is not wheel friendly). For a more scenic route, venture past the butterfly garden and into the woods, which will eventually lead you to the canal path.

Erie Canal Heritage Trail

13

100 KENTUCKY AVE, ROCHESTER, NY 14606

LIONS PARK

SUMMARY

Lions Park features a fun and colorful playground containing a rock wall and several unique bridges and ladders. The playground is situated a good distance from the parking lot and water. Across from the playground, you'll discover a large sandbox and plenty of swings. Don't forget to bring sand toys for the sandbox!

EXTEND THE TRIP

You can extend your trip by taking a stroll or bike ride around the 1/3-mile paved loop that encircles the park and stopping by Trolley Pond to observe the wildlife. If you veer off the path at the woodline, you'll reach Gates Memorial Park, where you can visit another playground! It's less than 1/4 mile to walk to this second park, and the walk is wheel-friendly. You'll also find a seasonal bathroom shelter there.

Gates Memorial Park
160 Spencerport Rd, Rochester, NY 14606

PLAYGROUND DETAILS

Condition: Good

Surface: Mulch

Shade: Some shaded green space surrounding playground, sandbox is shaded

Sand Play: Yes

Water Play: No

Picnic: Picnic tables under pavilion when not in use or picnic under the shade of a tree

Creeks/Lakes: Pond at the back of park

Wheel Friendly Features: Paved path circles the park

Cost: Free

SWINGS
Regular: 4
Adaptive: 0
Baby: 4
Tire: 0
Tandem: 0

3 VINCE TOFANY BLVD, ROCHESTER, NY 14612

KIDS CANYON PLAYGROUND

PLAYGROUND DETAILS

Condition: Good

Surface: Rubber (playground), cement (splash pad)

Shade: None

Sand Play: No

Water Play: Splash pad nearby

Picnic: There's a couple of picnic tables outside the fence

Creeks/Lakes: Pond nearby

Wheel Friendly Features: Zero grade entry to rubber surface playground with wide spacing between structures

Cost: Playground is free, there is a fee for non-residents to use the splash pad

SWINGS
Regular: 4
Adaptive: 0
Baby: 1
Tire: 0
Tandem: 1

SUMMARY

This playground/splash pad combo is designed for younger children and will surely spark their imagination with its outdoor/animal theme. It features large fish, beavers, and bears to climb on, along with a variety of swing types, making it suitable for various needs and abilities. The play area is fenced in, nicely padded, very clean, and well-maintained.

EXTEND THE TRIP

The playground is within walking distance of the Greece Community Center and Library. The Greece Public Library has renovated its children's area, creating the Story Garden, a multi-room (and multi-level) play area for children of all ages. Alongside their children's books and resources, the space includes a giant light bright, a play grocery store area, a fairy tree ball chute, and much more.

Greece Public Library
2 Vince Tofany Blvd, Rochester, NY 14612

15 LONG POND RD, ROCHESTER, NY 14612

GOODWIN PARK

SUMMARY

This playground in Greece offers plenty of fun with numerous opportunities for scaling, climbing, and sliding. A unique and beloved feature is the large spider web. While there are aspects that toddlers may enjoy, due to the nearby road, open water, and climbing features, this playground is best suited for older kids and those who do well with boundaries.

EXTEND THE TRIP

Drive just 4 minutes down to Moon Beach for a stroll and some sand play! You can enter through the Braddock Bay Marina entrance for parking. Alternatively, you can use the Braddock Bay Park entrance at 199 E Manitou Rd. to visit the Hawk watch tower and take a stroll along the bay.

Braddock Beach/Moon Beach
189 Braddock Rd, Rochester, NY 14612

PLAYGROUND DETAILS

Condition: New, built in 2022

Surface: Mulch

Shade: Some shaded green space surrounding playground

Sand Play: No

Water Play: No

Picnic: Single picnic table

Creeks/Lakes: Lake Ontario inlet parallels playground

Wheel Friendly Features: None

Cost: Free

SWINGS
Regular: 0
Adaptive: 0
Baby: 0
Tire: 0
Tandem: 0

4614 DEWEY AVE, ROCHESTER, NY 14612

VETERANS PARK

PLAYGROUND DETAILS

Condition: New, built in 2023

Surface: Mulch

Shade: None

Sand Play: No

Water Play: No

Picnic: Pavilion with picnic tables directly behind playground

Creeks/Lakes: None

Wheel Friendly Features: None

Cost: Free

SWINGS
Regular: 4
Adaptive: 0
Baby: 2
Tire: 0
Tandem: 0

SUMMARY

The new playground at Veterans Park in Greece is small but mighty and designed for the littlest of playground enthusiasts, aged 6-23 months, with close supervision. Even though it's intended for little ones, the playground also features a gaga pit on-site, as well as regular swings that older kids can enjoy.

EXTEND THE TRIP

Bring a friend and go for a hike! The trails at Veterans Park lead to the playground at Badgerow Park South. The hike from one playground to the other is approximately 1/4 mile. Visit the Town of Greece's website and search for the 'Veterans Park Trail Map' to explore various hiking options within the park.

Trail head behind playground

17

955 ENGLISH RD, ROCHESTER, NY 14616

BASIL MARELLA PARK

SUMMARY

Adjacent to an older playground at Basil Marella Park, you'll find the newly built, fenced-in, inclusive playground. This barrier-free section of the park was established in August 2021 and features a We-Go-Round, sensory center, and a We-Go-Swing (one of the first in the country!). There are numerous unique elements here, well-spaced out, providing ample room for inclusive play.

PLAYGROUND DETAILS

Condition: New, built in 2021 and in excellent condition

Surface: Cement

Shade: None

Sand Play: No

Water Play: No

Picnic: Pavilion with picnic tables nearby

Creeks/Lakes: Creek parallels hiking trail

Wheel Friendly Features: Zero grade entry to rubber surface, zero grade entry "We-go-round," ADA compliment restrooms.

Cost: Free

EXTEND THE TRIP

If you follow the paved path from the playground away from the parking lot, you'll come across a nicely wooded trail lined with fitness equipment. The entire path is paved and therefore wheel-friendly. This path is part of the Rte 390 Trail and continues on for several miles without looping. You will likely encounter dog walkers, bicyclists and more using this path, though it is wide so there is room for everyone!

SWINGS
Regular: 2
Adaptive: 2
Baby: 0
Tire: 0
Tandem: 0

Basil Marella Park Fitness Trail

461 BONESTEEL ST, GREECE, NY 14616

COLUMBUS PARK

PLAYGROUND DETAILS

Condition: Good, built in 2020

Surface: Mulch

Shade: Playground is in direct sun, shade in surrounding green space

Sand Play: No

Water Play: No

Picnic: Much green space for a picnic blanket

Creeks/Lakes: None

Wheel Friendly Features: None

Cost: Free

SWINGS
Regular: 3
Adaptive: 1
Baby: 2
Tire: 0
Tandem: 0

SUMMARY

This Greece playground offers a variety of swings, including typical, baby, and adaptive swings, as well as numerous structures suitable for both young and older kids. The design is visually appealing, featuring faux logs, tree structures, and hidden animals throughout. You can pack a lunch and bring a picnic blanket, as there are open fields with plenty of shade right next to the playground. Note, the playground is close to the parking lot.

EXTEND THE TRIP

Worked up an appetite from all that playing? Donuts Delite is just a 3-minute drive from Columbus Park! They are open 7 days a week from 6:00 AM to 2:00 PM, serving donuts, breakfast, and Salvatore's pizza. You'll find indoor and outdoor seating available.

Donuts Delite
674 W Ridge Rd, Rochester, NY 14615

HAWK SHELTER: ZOO RD, ROCHESTER, NY 14617

SENECA PARK

SUMMARY

Did you know that Seneca Park has two playgrounds outside the zoo? The second playground can be found by taking Zoo Road past the zoo and following the one-way road around to Hawk Shelter. This playground is nicely shaded and features unique animal statues. While the play area itself is small, kids will be entertained with the large camel and elephant to climb on, as well as the vast amount of space to explore.

EXTEND THE TRIP

If you're local to Rochester, you're likely familiar with the Seneca Park Zoo. With membership or daily admission options available, it's a popular spot to spend time outside. You can see animals such as elephants, giraffes, zebras, rhinos, sea lions, otters, penguins, lions, wolves, tigers, red pandas, snow leopards, and more. The trails are wide and stroller-friendly, and the walk is there and back, totaling about 1.3 miles.

Seneca Park Zoo
2222 St Paul St, Rochester, NY 14621

PLAYGROUND DETAILS

Condition: Fair

Surface: Mulch

Shade: Yes

Sand Play: No

Water Play: No

Picnic: Pavilion with picnic tables nearby

Creeks/Lakes: Hiking opportunities to see Genesee River and waterfall, as well as a pond nearby with a variety of waterfowl

Wheel Friendly Features: None

Cost: Free

SWINGS
Regular: 2
Adaptive: 0
Baby: 2
Tire: 0
Tandem: 0

1558 LAKESHORE BLVD., IRONDEQUOIT, ROCHESTER, NY 14617

CAMP EASTMAN

PLAYGROUND DETAILS

Condition: Fair, keep an eye out for construction in Spring 2024

Surface: Rubber (playground), cement (splash pad)

Shade: Partially shaded playground and surrounding green space

Sand Play: No

Water Play: Splash pad

Picnic: Small pavilion nearby with picnic tables

Creeks/Lakes: Lake Ontario a short drive away

Wheel Friendly Features: Zero grade entry to rubber surface and splash pad, ramp up play structure

Cost: Free

SWINGS
Regular: 2
Adaptive: 1
Baby: 1
Tire: 0
Tandem: 0

SUMMARY

Camp Eastman provides a secluded splash pad and a playground that's open and free to the public. The playground is spacious, offering plenty of room for children to play. It is considered 'barrier-free' and includes an adaptive swing, ramps, and a path of percussion instruments. You'll also find a rocking boat structure, roundabout, and spring car here.

EXTEND THE TRIP

If the splash pad isn't enough, you can cool off at the beach just across the street! The beach at Durand Eastman is expansive and perfect for playing in the sand. Swimming is supervised by beach guards in its designated area (Lot A), and lifeguards are on duty from 12:00 – 6:00 p.m. seven days a week during the summer. Before heading out, call the Monroe County Beach Hotline at (585) 753-5887 for beach conditions.

Durand Eastman Beach
1342 Lakeshore Blvd, Rochester, NY 14622

LOG CABIN RD, ROCHESTER, NY 14622
DURAND EASTMAN PARK

SUMMARY
This Durand Eastman playground is located at the end of Log Cabin Road, across from the beach. Situated at the road's end, the playground is surrounded by woods, offering both shade and seclusion. Several pavilions with picnic tables and grills nearby make it an excellent spot for a cookout!

PLAYGROUND DETAILS

Condition: Good

Surface: Mulch

Shade: Yes

Sand Play: No

Water Play: No

Picnic: Pavilions with picnic tables and grills nearby

Creeks/Lakes: Lake Ontario is down the road

Wheel Friendly Features: None

Cost: Free

EXTEND THE TRIP
The Durand Eastman Park Arboretum is a must-visit, especially in the Spring and Fall. It's just a quick 4-minute drive from the playground. This is an ideal spot for an easy stroll with the kids or the dog. The vast green space and well-maintained grounds provide a beautiful area for picnics and exploring nature. There's a large variety of unique trees, and the rolling hills are perfect for running up and down!

Durand Eastman Park Arboretum
Pine Valley Rd, Rochester, NY 14622

SWINGS
Regular: 2
Adaptive: 0
Baby: 2
Tire: 0
Tandem: 0

RUDMAN RD, IRONDEQUOIT, NY 14622

HEYER-BAYER MEMORIAL PARK

PLAYGROUND DETAILS

Condition: New, built in 2022

Surface: Rubber

Shade: No

Sand Play: No

Water Play: No

Picnic: 1 picnic table

Creeks/Lakes: None

Wheel Friendly Features: Zero grade entry to rubber surface, ramps to play structure, zero grade entry merry go round.

Cost: Free

SWINGS
Regular: 2
Adaptive: 1
Baby: 1
Tire: 0
Tandem: 0

SUMMARY

The new inclusive playground at Heyer-Bayer Memorial Park is rubber-surfaced and offers something for a wide range of ages and abilities. You'll find a variety of swings, an adaptive modern merry-go-round, a roller slide, climbing features, unique monkey bars, sensory boards, and more. There is a secure fence between the playground and the busy road, although it doesn't encompass the entire playground.

EXTEND THE TRIP

This playground is a pleasant stop on your way to Seabreeze. If you find yourself running ahead of schedule, you can pass the time here while waiting for the amusement park to open.

Planning to playground hop instead? Irondequoit Bay Marine Park is just a few minutes down the road. For more details, refer to the next page!

Seabreeze Amusement Park
4600 Culver Rd, Rochester, NY 14622

1 SECRET COVE PARK PARK, ROCHESTER, NY 14622

IRONDEQUOIT BAY MARINE PARK

SUMMARY
This is one of the few fully fenced-in and gated playgrounds in the area, offering long-lasting entertainment. Kids adore the pirate-themed play structure and the 'trirunner' (pictured). There's plenty to do for a wide range of ages! Bathrooms can be found nearby if patronizing local businesses or down the road near the beach.

EXTEND THE TRIP
Take a 5-10 minute stroller-friendly walk or a 2-minute drive to the end of Culver Road to reach the Irondequoit Bay Outlet Pier and Beach. While swimming is not permitted here, it's a fun spot to play in the sand, dip your toes in the water, or walk the pier. Along the way, you'll find several spots to stop for food or ice cream!

Irondequoit Bay Outlet Pier and Beach
4993 Culver Rd, Rochester, NY 14622

PLAYGROUND DETAILS

Condition: New, built in 2021

Surface: Mulch

Shade: No

Sand Play: No

Water Play: No

Picnic: Pavilion with picnic tables nearby, alternatively, Bill Gray's is just steps away

Creeks/Lakes: Lake Ontario is just across the street

Wheel Friendly Features: Wide paved path from playground to beach

Cost: Free

SWINGS
Regular: 4
Adaptive: 2
Baby: 0
Tire: 0
Tandem: 0

302 LAKE RD, WEBSTER, NY 14580

SANDBAR PARK

PLAYGROUND DETAILS

Condition: Excellent, built in 2023

Surface: Mulch

Shade: None

Sand Play: No

Water Play: No

Picnic: No picnic tables, limited benches

Creeks/Lakes: Playground is adjacent to Lake Ontario.

Wheel Friendly Features: Wide paved path along lake

Cost: Free

SWINGS
Regular: 0
Adaptive: 1
Baby: 0
Tire: 2
Tandem: 0

SUMMARY

What a delightful space! Sandbar Park was established with the goal of preserving the area for future generations. The playground offers a variety of activities, including climbing and balancing structures for kids aged 5 and up, as well as swings and a unique slide for the little ones. Right off the playground, there's a nicely paved walkway for a leisurely stroll after playing. Be sure to layer up, as there's often a pleasant breeze from the lake here.

EXTEND THE TRIP

There are ample hiking opportunities in this area of Webster. A 4-minute drive will take you to Vosburg Hollow. Alternatively, 10 minutes down the road, you'll find Webster Park and Four Mile Creek Preserve. Each of these hiking opportunities features a creek running through them, with the creek at Webster Park and Four Mile Creek being particularly inviting!

Four Mile Creek Preserve
1433-1439 Lake Rd, Webster, NY 14580

LAKE RD & HOLT RD WEBSTER, NY 14580

JACK'S PLACE, WEBSTER PARK

SUMMARY

This playground is a paradise for dinosaur lovers! It features multiple levels, making it perfect for various age groups. Even when the park gets busy, there is ample space to enjoy. The playground's proximity to the lake provides a pleasant breeze. You'll find an outhouse a short walk from the playground, and although a bit of a walk, there are seasonal restrooms across the street.

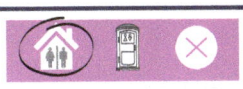

PLAYGROUND DETAILS

Condition: Excellent

Surface: Mulch

Shade: None

Sand Play: No

Water Play: No

Picnic: Limited
Picnic tables near playground, several tables and grills throughout the park.

Creeks/Lakes: Lake Ontario and Mill Creek are a short drive away

Wheel Friendly Features: None

Cost: Free

EXTEND THE TRIP

After enjoying the playground, you can take a stroll through the park or drive down the road to reach Webster Pier. If you're up for a longer walk, you can cross Holt Road from the playground and walk through the park to find Mill Creek. From there, you can follow the creek to the lake.

Webster Pier
1100 Lake Rd, Webster, NY 14580

SWINGS
Regular: 4
Adaptive: 1
Baby: 1
Tire: 0
Tandem: 0

1700 SCHLEGEL RD, WEBSTER, NY 14580

KENT PARK

PLAYGROUND DETAILS

Condition: Good

Surface: Rubber mulch

Shade: Pavilion nearby and surrounding trees provide shade in green space

Sand Play: No

Water Play: No

Picnic: Several picnic tables under pavilion

Creeks/Lakes: Small creek within arboretum

Wheel Friendly Features: Arboretum paths are wheel friendly

Cost: Free

SWINGS
Regular: 0
Adaptive: 2
Baby: 0
Tire: 0
Tandem: 0

SUMMARY

his is a wonderful playground with abundant natural beauty. It offers numerous opportunities for climbing and features many slides of various lengths. Benches are conveniently placed in the shade. However, what truly makes this park special is the arboretum. Be sure to pack a lunch and take a stroll through it!

EXTEND THE TRIP

The Webster Arboretum offers a truly beautiful stroll throughout the year, and entrance is free. It can be accessed by walking behind the playground and crossing the bridge. Some paths are paved, while others are gravel, but all are stroller-friendly. Just be aware that it can get muddy after heavy rainfall. Keep a close eye out for butterflies and other wildlife, and be sure to visit in the spring when the lilacs, magnolias, and many other flowering plants are in full bloom.

Webster Arboretum
1700 Schlegel Rd, Webster, NY 14580

1350 CHIYODA DR, WEBSTER, NY 14580

FIRST RESPONDERS PARK

SUMMARY

This firefighter-themed playground and splash pad provide hours of fun. A pavilion is conveniently located between the splash pad and playground, offering a shaded area for resting and picnicking. The playground and splash pad are situated away from the road, and they are close enough to each other for children to easily run back and forth.

EXTEND THE TRIP

The Webster Recreation Center provides numerous events and affordable family fun options. A unique fitness area can be found behind the center. To get there, take a walk along the Chiyoda Trail from the Recreation Center parking lot to the fitness area behind the baseball fields. The walk is just under 1/3 mile. Once there, you'll discover a parkour-style fitness zone, offering entertainment and challenges for kids and adults. It features a climbing wall, tunnels, a tire course, balance beams, and more."

Webster Recreation Fitness Area

PLAYGROUND DETAILS

Condition: Good

Surface: Rubber (playground), cement (splash pad)

Shade: Playground and splash pad in direct sun, large pavilion for shade

Sand Play: No

Water Play: Splash pad

Picnic: Several picnic tables under pavilion

Creeks/Lakes: None

Wheel Friendly Features: Zero grade entry splash pad and playground, wheel friendly surfaces, ramp on one play structure

Cost: Free

SWINGS
Regular: 2
Adaptive: 1
Baby: 1
Tire: 0
Tandem: 0

VAN INGEN DR, WEBSTER, NY 14580

KARPUS FAMILY PLAYGROUND

PLAYGROUND DETAILS

Condition: Excellent

Surface: Rubber

Shade: Playground in direct sun, pavilion within fenced-in area for shade

Sand Play: No

Water Play: No

Picnic: Picnic tables under pavilion

Creeks/Lakes: None

Wheel Friendly Features: Zero grade entry, ramps to play structure, zero grade roundabout

Cost: Free

SWINGS
Regular: 4
Adaptive: 2
Baby: 2
Tire: 0
Tandem: 1

SUMMARY

The playground at Ridge Park offers wheelchair accessibility and fun for all. The rubber play surface is not only great for wheelchairs but also for crawling kiddos. The ramps and bridges are wide and open, and there is a communication board on-site. Please note that this playground is adjacent to Miracle Field, so it may get busy on game days.

EXTEND THE TRIP

Just down the street from Ridge Park, you'll find the delightful and allergen-friendly ice cream shop, Bruster's! They offer a wide range of ice cream choices for the whole family, and kids 40" and under get a free kids cone.

If you'd prefer to skip the ice cream, you can take a short walk to Webster Library from the playground to cool off in their beautiful children's section.

Bruster's Real Ice Cream
1041 Ridge Rd Sr404, Webster, NY 14580

29

1559 EMPIRE BLVD, WEBSTER, NY 14580

ABRAHAM LINCOLN PARK

SUMMARY

Abraham Lincoln Park has something for everyone. Upon entering, you'll find a typical playground, but if you walk further, you'll soon discover a natural log playground in the shade. Both playgrounds cater to a wide range of ages, and kids will particularly enjoy the log cabin and tunnels here!

PLAYGROUND DETAILS

Condition: Good, the natural playground has been updated in 2023

Surface: Mulch

Shade: Natural play area is shaded

Sand Play: No

Water Play: No

Picnic: Two small pavilions with a picnic table in each

Creeks/Lakes: There is a creek and views of Irondequoit Bay along the hiking trail

Wheel Friendly Features: None

Cost: Free

EXTEND THE TRIP

Take a hike! The trails at Abraham Lincoln Park feature rolling terrain and some steep hills, making them more suitable for older kids. You can walk alongside the bay, which offers beautiful views but also steep drops along the trail's edge. There are trailheads on either side of the natural playground, and both will lead you to the path at the bottom of the hill.

SWINGS
Regular: 0
Adaptive: 0
Baby: 0
Tire: 0
Tandem: 0

1648 FIVE MILE LINE RD, PENFIELD, NY 14526

JACK'S PLACE, ROTHFUSS PARK

PLAYGROUND DETAILS

Condition: Good

Surface: Mulch

Shade: None

Sand Play: Yes

Water Play: No

Picnic: Limited picnic tables under small pavilion, plenty of green space for picnic blanket

Creeks/Lakes: None

Wheel Friendly Features: None at the Jack's Place playground but wide paved path lead to the second playground within Rothfuss Park that is fully accessible

Cost: Free

SWINGS
Regular: 2
Adaptive: 0
Baby: 2
Tire: 0
Tandem: 0

Adaptive swing and tandem swing can be found at second playground

SUMMARY

Rothfuss Park is a beautiful and popular park in Penfield, boasting two beloved playgrounds. Jack's Place is a unique dinosaur-themed playground with a large sandbox where kids can dig for dinosaur bones using shovels, brushes, and other toys. Please note that the bathroom is a bit of a walk from the playground and is seasonal. This park often attracts a large but friendly crowd.

EXTEND THE TRIP

Rothfuss Park features wide paved paths throughout the park, making it convenient to bring bikes or scooters for an easy trip to the bathroom or the second playground. The second playground is filled with inclusive features, including musical instruments and a tandem swing with an adaptive seat.

Inclusive playground within Rothfuss Park

1628 JACKSON RD, PENFIELD, NY 14526

VETERANS MEMORIAL PARK

SUMMARY

This playground features bridges, slides, and fun ways to reach them. However, what makes this playground unique is the neighboring Tot Trail! The Tot Trail is a short, stroller-friendly path near the playground, offering a variety of climbing and balancing structures. Much of the trail is shaded!

PLAYGROUND DETAILS

Condition: Good

Surface: Mulch

Shade: Playground in sun, tot trail partially shaded

Sand Play: No

Water Play: No

Picnic: Limited picnic tables nearby, plenty of surrounding green space for a picnic blanket

Creeks/Lakes: None

Wheel Friendly Features: Wide paved path along the tot trail and throughout park

Cost: Free

SWINGS
Regular: 2
Adaptive: 1
Baby: 1
Tire: 0
Tandem: 0

EXTEND THE TRIP

Take a short drive down Jackson Road to reach Thousand Acre Swamp for a unique hiking experience. It features a beautiful boardwalk and abundant wildlife to spot. This is a 2.9-mile out-and-back trail, but there's an opportunity to loop back after the boardwalk, making the trail much shorter. The trail is considered easy but not wheel friendly. The swamp is one of Monroe County's largest wetland systems. Please note that dogs are not allowed.

Thousand Acre Swamp
1587 Jackson Rd Penfield, NY 14526.

32

100 E IVY ST, EAST ROCHESTER, NY 14445
EDMUND LYON PARK SPLASHPAD

PLAYGROUND DETAILS

Condition: Good

Surface: Cement

Shade: Direct sun, limited shade sails

Sand Play: No

Water Play: Splash pad

Picnic: Limited picnic tables and grills near splash pad

Creeks/Lakes: None

Wheel Friendly Features: Zero grade entry to splash pad, paved paths throughout park

Cost: Free

SWINGS
Regular: 8
Adaptive: 0
Baby: 4
Tire: 0
Tandem: 0

at nearby playground

SUMMARY

The splash pad is the highlight of Edmund Lyon Park when visiting with kids. While there is a playground here, it is in poor condition. The splash pad has a pirate theme with moving water cannons and a small slide for toddlers. The splash pad surface can be slippery, so it's advisable to wear water shoes or sandals. Although there is a bathroom on site, it's located on the other side of the park, so it's probably easiest to come with the kids dressed and ready to go!

EXTEND THE TRIP

You can extend the trip by visiting the playground, taking a stroll through the park, or heading over to the East Rochester Public Library. The library is just a 5-minute walk or a 2-minute drive from Edmund Lyon Park and offers a children's section with a toy kitchen, blocks, puzzles, and more!

East Rochester Public Library
317 Main St, East Rochester, NY 14445

33

99 O'CONNOR RD, FAIRPORT, NY 14450

PERINTON PARK

SUMMARY

This playground is a local favorite due to its spacious layout, ample shade, and variety of swings. It offers separate areas for different age groups and is set back from the road, parking lot, and canal. After playing, enjoy watching kayaks and ducks pass by at the nearby canal!

PLAYGROUND DETAILS

Condition: Good

Surface: Partially rubber, mostly mulch

Shade: Partial

Sand Play: No

Water Play: No

Picnic: Grills and picnic tables throughout park

Creeks/Lakes: Erie Canal located at the back of park

Wheel Friendly Features: Paved paths throughout park and along the Erie Canal Heritage trail, small ramp leads to percussion instruments on play structure

Cost: Free

SWINGS
Regular: 8
Adaptive: 1
Baby: 6
Tire: 0
Tandem: 0

EXTEND THE TRIP

Perinton Park is located along the Erie Canal Heritage Trail. You can walk along the paved path or, after passing under the bridge, follow the sidewalk to Tom Wahl's for a milkshake or meal. Additionally, the park offers grills and picnic tables, making it a great spot for a canal-side meal.

Tom Wahl's Fairport
1333 Fairport Rd, Fairport, NY 14450

34

499 FELLOWS RD, FAIRPORT, NY 14450

FELLOWS ROAD PARK

PLAYGROUND DETAILS

Condition: Good

Surface: Turf and mulch

Shade: Shade sail over some of the playground, shade in surrounding green space

Sand Play: No

Water Play: No

Picnic: Limited grills and picnic tables

Creeks/Lakes: None

Wheel Friendly Features: Fitness trail is wheel friendly

Cost: Free

SWINGS
Regular: 2
Adaptive: 0
Baby: 2
Tire: 0
Tandem: 0

SUMMARY

Fellows Road Park offers a wide array of structured recreation, including soccer, volleyball, basketball, tennis, pickleball, and softball. The playground features unique play structures like a firetruck and school bus. It includes areas with wood chip and artificial turf surfacing. Note, the playground is fairly close to the parking lot but has a lot of open space and fields behind it. If you are looking to burn some energy, this is a great spot to go!

EXTEND THE TRIP

The fitness trail is a highlight of the park and a fantastic way for the entire family to engage in physical activity. Bring a stroller for the little one and bikes for the older kids, and enjoy a fun workout while stopping at the various exercise stations along the nearly 1-mile loop that encircles the park.

Fitness trail at Fellows Road Park

1100 AYRAULT RD, FAIRPORT, NY 14450

CENTER PARK WEST

SUMMARY

Center Park West features a spacious and popular playground catering to various age groups. It includes a tall, thrilling slide for older kids and a designated area for younger ones. Note, a playground replacement is planned for 2025.

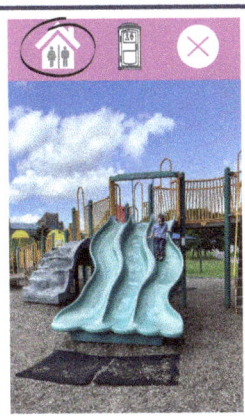

EXTEND THE TRIP

After playing on the playground, kids can take a walk along the path, which sometimes features a story path. If you're up for some light hiking, explore the wooded trails. The amphitheater is another enjoyable spot, especially during open-air concerts on Sundays in the summer. You can also time your visit with the Community Center's open gym or open swim hours; just check their website for the schedule and fees.

Perinton Community Center
1350 Turk Hill Rd, Fairport, NY 14450

PLAYGROUND DETAILS

Condition: Fair

Surface: Mulch

Shade: Playground in direct sun, shade sails available

Sand Play: No

Water Play: None at playground, aquatic center nearby (fees apply)

Picnic: Picnic tables available when shelter not in use

Creeks/Lakes: None

Wheel Friendly Features: Wide paved path through park

Cost: Free

SWINGS
Regular: 0
Adaptive: 0
Baby: 0
Tire: 0
Tandem: 0

36

99 VICTOR RD, FAIRPORT, NY 14450

EGYPT PARK

PLAYGROUND DETAILS

Condition: Good

Surface: Rubber

Shade: Playground in sun, nearby green space is shaded

Sand Play: No

Water Play: No

Picnic: There is a pavilion with picnic tables near by

Creeks/Lakes: None

Wheel Friendly Features: Zero grade entry to rubber surface, ramp to sensory features

Cost: Free

SWINGS
Regular: 2
Adaptive: 2
Baby: 2
Tire: 0
Tandem: 0

SUMMARY

Egypt Park is a crowd-pleaser with its farm-themed structures, including a tractor-shaped play area. It offers a diverse selection of swings and features wide ramps for easy accessibility. The playground is thoughtfully situated away from the parking area and road, providing ample green space for kids to run around.

EXTEND THE TRIP

You can access Lollypop Farm from Egypt Park via a path located just beyond the parking lot. After passing the boardwalk, head straight towards the closed gate leading to the Farm Walk area. You can open the gate to enter the Farm Walk section. The trails along the Farm Walk are wide, flat, and typically host several farm animals for visitors to observe. This trail is open year-round and can accommodate strollers, but be mindful that it can get muddy, especially during wet conditions.

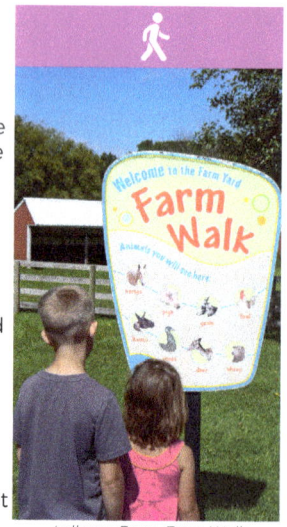

Lollypop Farm, Farm Walk
99 Victor Rd, Fairport, NY 14450

555 KREAG RD, PITTSFORD, NY 14534

KREAG ROAD PARK

SUMMARY

Kreag Road Park is one of the few local playgrounds equipped with a stocked, shaded sandbox for children to enjoy. In addition, the park features a new modern playground, tennis courts, basketball courts, softball fields, and offers a view of the Erie Canal.

EXTEND THE TRIP

Abbott's Frozen Custard is just a quick 2-minute drive from Kreag Road Park. This charming location sits alongside the canal, allowing you to grab a cone and take a leisurely stroll along the water. For the more adventurous, there are sidewalks connecting Kreag Road Park to this Abbott's location, offering the option of a 12-minute walk there as well!

Abbott's Frozen Custard
624 Pittsford Victor Rd, Pittsford, NY 14534

PLAYGROUND DETAILS

Condition: New, built in 2023

Surface: Mulch

Shade: The playground is not shaded but the sandbox and surrounding green space is

Sand Play: Yes

Water Play: No

Picnic: Several picnic tables and a pavilion

Creeks/Lakes: The canal is approximately 100 yards behind the playground

Wheel Friendly Features: None

Cost: Free

SWINGS
Regular: 2
Adaptive: 1
(Adaptive Tandem Swing)
Baby: 1
Tire: 0
Tandem: 1

43 WOOLSTON ROAD, PITTSFORD, NY
POWDER MILLS PARK

PLAYGROUND DETAILS

Condition: Excellent, built in 2023

Surface: Mulch

Shade: No

Sand Play: No

Water Play: No

Picnic: Limited picnic tables and benches near playground

Creeks/Lakes: Irondequoit creek winds throughout the park but not close to playground

Wheel Friendly Features: None

Cost: Free

SWINGS
Regular: 2
Adaptive: 0
Baby: 2
Tire: 0
Tandem: 0

SUMMARY

This brand new playground perfectly complements the park's theme. You'll discover frog, fish, and turtle structures for climbing, along with numerous other climbing features and slides. There are two separate play areas, one designed for older kids and another dedicated to the little ones. This playground also boasts the beloved "trirunner" (refer to page 24 for details on a second trirunner location).

EXTEND THE TRIP

The Powder Mills Fish Hatchery is an enjoyable experience for all ages. You can feed fish at various stages of life by bringing along a cup and some quarters for fish food. The park provides several coin-operated feed machines near the holding areas. The Fish Hatchery is accessible for strollers and wheelchairs. Additionally, there's a trail behind the hatchery (not wheel friendly) and a nearby creek for further exploration.

Powder Mills Fish Hatchery
115 Park Rd, Pittsford, NY 14534

480 MENDON RD, PITTSFORD, NY 14534

THORNELL FARM PARK

SUMMARY

The playground at Thornell Farm Park boasts numerous distinctive structures that set it apart from others, including a variety of bridges, buttons, and rock walls. This playground is quite spacious, suitable for all ages, and is often populated with other children to play with.

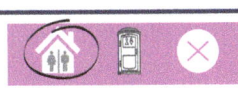

PLAYGROUND DETAILS

Condition: Good

Surface: Mulch

Shade: Shade in some surrounding green space and nearby pavilion

Sand Play: No

Water Play: No

Picnic: Picnic tables can be found at nearby pavilion

Creeks/Lakes: None

Wheel Friendly Features: Paved path leads to short playground ramp that stops at the steering wheels and other manipulatives, paths in park are wheel friendly.

Cost: Free

SWINGS
Regular: 4
Adaptive: 2
Baby: 2
Tire: 0
Tandem: 0

EXTEND THE TRIP

Thornell Farm Park offers plenty of opportunities for physical activity. In addition to the playground, there is a 0.78-mile stone trail that encircles the park, as well as other paved paths leading to the athletic fields. Consider bringing bikes to explore the park further and extend your visit!

0.78-mile fitness loop at Thornell Farm Park

629 MARSH RD, PITTSFORD, NY 14534

GREAT EMBANKMENT PARK

PLAYGROUND DETAILS

Condition: Excellent

Surface: Mulch

Shade: No

Sand Play: No

Water Play: No

Picnic: Pavilion with picnic tables

Creeks/Lakes: Canal towards back of park

Wheel Friendly Features: None

Cost: Free

SWINGS
Regular: 4
Adaptive: 1
Baby: 1
Tire: 0
Tandem: 0

SUMMARY

Great Embankment Park is a spacious park that offers a variety of activities. It's frequently used for soccer, softball, and baseball games and is known for its extensive green space and open fields. Note, to get to the playground, you'll need to walk up a steep hill or across the length of a soccer field.

EXTEND THE TRIP

Powers Farm Market is a beloved local farm that offers fresh produce and a wide range of animals to interact with. It's conveniently located just 4 minutes down the road from Great Embankment Park. At Powers Farm Market, you can find food dispensers to feed the animals, and if you visit in the fall, you won't want to miss the famous Powers tepees. There's no cost to enter the farm market, see the animals, and explore the teepees.

Powers Farm Market
161 Marsh Rd, Pittsford, NY 14534

41

35 LINCOLN AVE, PITTSFORD, NY 14534

PITTSFORD COMMUNITY CENTER

SUMMARY

The Pittsford Community Center boasts a shaded playground with unique play structures. One of the highlights of this playground is the lion-shaped structure and the story walk. The playground is situated right behind the community center, making it convenient for families. You can find bathrooms inside the community center when it's open. For added fun, consider registering for the Parent and Tot open Gym session before heading to the playground!

PLAYGROUND DETAILS

Condition: Good

Surface: Mulch

Shade: Partial

Sand Play: No

Water Play: No

Picnic: Limited picnic tables

Creeks/Lakes: None

Wheel Friendly Features: None

Cost: Free

EXTEND THE TRIP

You can follow the sidewalks from the Community Center to the charming Village of Pittsford. Once in the village, you have a variety of options for dining, shopping, enjoying ice cream, or having a cup of coffee at one of the many local businesses. Additionally, you can visit the Pittsford Library, or take a leisurely stroll along the scenic canal at Schoen Place, which is a short 3-minute drive or a pleasant 12-minute walk from the Community Center playground.

Schoen Place
Schoen Pl, Pittsford, NY 14534

SWINGS
Regular: 2
Adaptive: 0
Baby: 2
Tire: 1
Tandem: 0

595 CALKINS RD, HENRIETTA, NY 14467

VETERANS MEMORIAL PARK

PLAYGROUND DETAILS

Condition: Fair

Surface: Mulch

Shade: Playground in direct sun, pavilions nearby and much shade in surrounding green spaces

Sand Play: No

Water Play: No

Picnic: Several pavilions, picnic tables and grills

Creeks/Lakes: None

Wheel Friendly Features: None

Cost: Free

SWINGS
Regular: 8
Adaptive: 0
Baby: 5
Tire: 1
Tandem: 0

SUMMARY

This is a large and highly popular playground with three separate structures to cater to different age groups. The first structure is designed for the youngest of children, featuring a wide platform and short slides. The second structure is slightly more advanced, offering a small rock wall and tunnel slide. The largest play structure is the main attraction and is enjoyed by a wide range of ages, featuring a climbing rock, tall slides, and bridges for added excitement.

EXTEND THE TRIP

The playground is located behind the Henrietta Recreation Center and library. In addition to this playground, there's a second one behind the recreation center. Inside the library, you'll find a fantastic children's section with various activities, such as a train table, puzzles, an expansive kitchen play area, as well as toy dinosaurs and a dollhouse inside a giant tree, all of which are sure to delight young visitors.

Henrietta Public Library
625 Calkins Rd, Rochester, NY 14623

43

DOUGLAS RD, PITTSFORD, NY 14534

MENDON PONDS PARK

SUMMARY

The playground at Mendon Ponds Park, located off Douglas Rd. near Hundred Acre Pond, offers various play equipment, including a spring car, standard swings, baby swings, and a delightful train-themed structure. There are two separate play areas suitable for different age groups. Seasonal restrooms are available near the playground, and just over the hill, you'll find a large pond to explore. During the winter, this area is a great spot for epic sledding adventures!

EXTEND THE TRIP

Mendon Ponds Park offers a diverse range of activities for a fun day out, from fishing and hiking to playground adventures, the nature center, the whimsical fairy trail, and the impressive birds of prey facility. It's a great place to connect with nature year-round. Consider packing a picnic and enjoying a full day of exploration. Keep in mind that some attractions within the park are a short drive away, like the Wild Wings Nature Center, which is approximately 7 minutes from the playground.

Wild Wings Nature Center
27 Pond Rd, Honeoye Falls, NY 14472

PLAYGROUND DETAILS

Condition: Fair

Surface: Mulch

Shade: Shade in surrounding green space

Sand Play: No

Water Play: No

Picnic: Pavilion with picnic tables a short walk from the playground

Creeks/Lakes: Hundred Acre Pond short walk away

Wheel Friendly Features: None

Cost: Free

SWINGS
Regular: 2
Adaptive: 0
Baby: 2
Tire: 0
Tandem: 0

44

108 SEMMEL RD, HONEOYE FALLS, NY 14472

DREISBACH SPLASH PARK

PLAYGROUND DETAILS

Condition: New, built in 2023

Surface: Cement

Shade: The splash pad is in direct sun, however there is a pavilion nearby for shade

Sand Play: No

Water Play: Splash pad

Picnic: Pavilion with picnic tables nearby

Creeks/Lakes: None

Wheel Friendly Features: Zero grade entry and accessible bathrooms

Cost: Free

SWINGS
Regular: 0
Adaptive: 0
Baby: 0
Tire: 0
Tandem: 0

SUMMARY

The splash pad at Semmel Road Park is a special place located near a military memorial dedicated to the memory of three New York State National Guardsmen. The splash pad is distinctive, featuring a large dumping bucket, water cannons, and various aquatic play structures like a crab and turtle. It's open daily from Memorial Day to Labor Day, providing a fun way for families to cool off during the summer months.

EXTEND THE TRIP

Just a short distance down the road at 95 Semmel Rd, you'll find a playground, courts, and hiking trails. The playground at Semmel Road Park is partially shaded, and it's located near the town's highway department, so kids might have the chance to spot some heavy equipment, which can be quite exciting. Additionally, you can extend the fun by exploring the fenced-in tennis and basketball courts, as well as the baseball field and walking paths through the woods.

Semmel Road Park Trails
95 Semmel Rd, Honeoye Falls, NY 14472

45

23 N MAIN ST, HONEOYE FALLS, NY 14472

HARRY ALLEN PARK

SUMMARY

This playground caters to various age groups with its well-maintained equipment, including baby swings, regular swings, spring toys, slides, and bridges. While there are no public restrooms on-site, you can find facilities at the nearby Mendon Library. Keep in mind that the playground is shared with a preschool, which can make it quite busy, especially during preschool hours. Nonetheless, it's a great spot for kids to enjoy.

EXTEND THE TRIP

The Mendon Public Library is a delightful addition to a day of exploring Honeoye Falls. Conveniently situated across the street from Harry Allen Park, it's a perfect stop for some family-friendly, free fun.

Alternatively, after visiting the playground, you can explore the nearby Zebulon Trail, which follows Honeoye Creek from Harry Allen Park to Rotary Park, where another fantastic playground awaits.

Mendon Public Library
22 N Main St, Honeoye Falls, NY 14472

PLAYGROUND DETAILS

Condition: Good

Surface: Mulch

Shade: None

Sand Play: No

Water Play: No

Picnic: Limited picnic tables

Creeks/Lakes: Honeoye Creek is along the Zebulon Norton Trail, the trailhead is a short walk from playground

Wheel Friendly Features: None

Cost: Free

SWINGS
Regular: 4
Adaptive: 0
Baby: 4
Tire: 0
Tandem: 0

46

1900 RUSH SCOTTSVILLE RD, RUSH, NY 14543

TOWN OF RUSH PLAYGROUND

PLAYGROUND DETAILS

Condition: Good

Surface: Mulch

Shade: None

Sand Play: No

Water Play: No

Picnic: Limited picnic tables and grills near playground

Creeks/Lakes: None

Wheel Friendly Features: None.

Cost: Free

SWINGS
Regular: 2
Adaptive: 0
Baby: 2
Tire: 0
Tandem: 0

SUMMARY

Discover the charming playground tucked away behind the Rush Public Library. Set away from the road, it offers a safe and fun space for children to play. With plenty of green space for running and separate structures catering to different age groups, this playground is sure to delight. Kids will enjoy the unique bridge leading to the slides and the small playhouse designed for the little ones.

EXTEND THE TRIP

A short and easy walk from the playground will take you to the Rush Public Library. Inside, you'll find the children's section, featuring a handful of children's computers and a wide selection of children's books. Don't miss the "Art Cart" for creative activities. The Rush Library is part of the Monroe County Library System and offers free entry for residents and non-residents. If you live outside of Monroe County, you can purchase a library card for a small annual fee to borrow materials. It's a great resource for both local and visiting families.

Rush Public Library
5977 E Henrietta Rd #9512, Rush, NY 14543

47

108 WESTCOMBE PARK, WEST HENRIETTA, NY 14586

BREESE PARK

SUMMARY

Breese Park is a hidden gem consisting of six small stations along a one-mile loop. Each station offers a unique element of play. To get to the park, you'll drive through a neighborhood, and once you arrive, follow the gravel path from the parking lot. Take the first right turn into the woods, and from there, follow left turns to stay on the fitness loop. This path is best suited for ages 3 and up, offering a delightful outdoor adventure for families.

EXTEND THE TRIP

GroMoore U-Pick Strawberries is a quick 5-minute drive from Breese Park. Visit in early June to enjoy 15-20 acres of pick-your-own strawberries. For more information, call the GroMoore Strawberry Hotline at (585) 533-1578. It's a delicious way to spend some quality time with your family while picking fresh, ripe strawberries

GroMoore U-Pick Strawberries
736 Rush Scottsville Rd, Rush, NY 14543

PLAYGROUND DETAILS

Condition: Excellent

Surface: Mulch

Shade: Yes

Sand Play: No

Water Play: No

Picnic: Limited picnic tables near the parking lot, plenty of open green space for a picnic blanket

Creeks/Lakes: Trail runs adjacent to the Genesee River

Wheel Friendly Features: None

Cost: Free

SWINGS
Regular: 0
Adaptive: 0
Baby: 0
Tire: 0
Tandem: 0

48

3835 UNION ST, NORTH CHILI, NY 14514

BLACK CREEK PARK

PLAYGROUND DETAILS

Condition: Good

Surface: Mulch

Shade: Shade in surrounding green space and nearby pavilion

Sand Play: No

Water Play: No

Picnic: Picnic tables and pavilion nearby

Creeks/Lakes: Pond a short walk away

Wheel Friendly Features: None

Cost: Free

SWINGS
Regular: 4
Adaptive: 0
Baby: 2
Tire: 0
Tandem: 0

SUMMARY

The playground at Black Creek Park is quite spacious and offers ample open space nearby for children to run and play. It features a variety of slides, bridges, and swings, making it an exciting play area for kids. The playground is also situated within a natural setting, providing the opportunity for additional exploration in the beautiful surroundings.

EXTEND THE TRIP

Black Creek Park is a spacious park that offers activities year-round. In the winter, you can enjoy sledding, and there are hiking opportunities throughout the year. Keep in mind that some of the trails can get muddy or swampy, so it's advisable to wear boots or sneakers. Starting from the playground, consider taking the Creek Trail, one of the park's five trails, to explore the pond and fields that lead to Black Creek.

Creek Trail at Black Creek Park

25 ROCK ISLAND RD, NORTH CHILI, NY 14514

UNION STATION PARK

SUMMARY

Union Station Park is a well-loved park that boasts a roomy splash pad and a playground designed for toddlers. During the summer, it's a popular spot for families looking to cool off on hot days. Be sure to bring cups, as kids can have fun filling them with water and dumping them into the drainage system. Keep in mind that the splash pad is in direct sunlight, so it's a good idea to bring sunhats and sunscreen.

PLAYGROUND DETAILS

Condition: Playground is in fair condition, splash pad is in excellent condition

Surface: Mulch (playground), cement (splash pad)

Shade: Direct sun with small pavilions nearby

Sand Play: No

Water Play: Splash pad

Picnic: Limited picnic tables

Creeks/Lakes: None

Wheel Friendly Features: Zero grade entry to the splash pad

Cost: Free

SWINGS
Regular: 5
Adaptive: 0
Baby: 3
Tire: 0
Tandem: 0

EXTEND THE TRIP

Union Station Park is a popular destination for its splash pad and playground, but it also offers a paved 3/4-mile loop right next to the playground. If you'd prefer a shorter walk, there's a shortcut available to create a 1/2-mile loop. The path, although narrow, isn't heavily trafficked, and it's free from roads and parking lots, making it a great place for kids to ride bikes, whether they're practicing or racing around.

Union Station Park track

50

269 OGDEN CENTER RD, SPENCERPORT, NY 14559

OGDEN TOWN OFFICES PARK

PLAYGROUND DETAILS

Condition: New, built in 2023

Surface: Rubber

Shade: Partial

Sand Play: No

Water Play: No

Picnic: Limited picnic tables

Creeks/Lakes: None

Wheel Friendly Features: Rubber surface playground and sidewalks to library, however you must cut through the grass to get to the playground

Cost: Free

SWINGS
Regular: 0
Adaptive: 0
Baby: 0
Tire: 0
Tandem: 0

SUMMARY

This newly constructed playground may be small in size, but it offers surprisingly enjoyable experiences. It features a rubber surface and a smaller play structure, making it an excellent space for younger children to explore. Additionally, there is a larger play structure with more challenging elements that older kids can enjoy. Restrooms are available inside the recreation center or library during their open hours.

EXTEND THE TRIP

The playground is situated within the same complex as the Ogden Farmers' Library. It's just a short walk or a quick drive across the parking lot. The library features a lovely children's section with an outdoor story garden that's accessible during the warmer months. You might even discover sand and bubbles to play with in this area!

Story Garden at Ogden Farmers' Library
269 Ogden Center Rd, Spencerport, NY 14559

99 PARK RD, SPENCERPORT, NY 14559

PINEWAY PONDS PARK

SUMMARY

The main attractions of Pineway Ponds Park are its splash pad and playground with a padded surface. The modern playground features a variety of climbing structures and a swing set with both typical and baby swings. The classic splash pad includes a large whale and sea lion fountain that children love to climb on, along with the cherished misting rainbow!

EXTEND THE TRIP

Just four-minute drive down the road lies the BrickLab, a fantastic destination for children and families alike. At the BrickLab, kids have the opportunity to unleash their creativity and imagination through free play with Legos, Duplos, and K'Nex. This innovative center caters to a broad spectrum of ages, thoughtfully designed with dedicated spaces for the littlest builders as well as areas that will challenge and engage even the most skilled and enthusiastic creators. Note, socks required! Check the open play schedule before heading out!

The BrickLab
5110 W Ridge Rd, Spencerport, NY 14559

PLAYGROUND DETAILS

Condition: Excellent

Surface: Rubber (playground), cement (splash pad)

Shade: Some shaded green space surrounding playground

Sand Play: No

Water Play: Splash pad

Picnic: Limited picnic tables near playground

Creeks/Lakes: None

Wheel Friendly Features: Zero grade entry to playground and splash pad

Cost: Free

SWINGS
Regular: 2
Adaptive: 0
Baby: 2
Tire: 0
Tandem: 0

52

1300 HILTON PARMA CORNERS RD, HILTON, NY 14468

ADVENTURE TOWERS PLAYGROUND

PLAYGROUND DETAILS

Condition: New, built in 2021

Surface: Rubber

Shade: None

Sand Play: No

Water Play: No

Picnic: Limited picnic tables near playground

Creeks/Lakes: There is a pond within the park, but not close to the playgrounds

Wheel Friendly Features: Zero grade entry to rubber surface and ramp to rocking boat apparatus

Cost: Free

SWINGS
Swings can be found at adjacent playground with mulch surface

SUMMARY

Adventure Towers Playground at Parma Town Park is an exciting and unique play area with a padded surface, towering slides, and challenging climbing nets. While it's suitable for a wide age range, it's recommended for children aged 5-12. After enjoying this playground, you can continue the fun at the second playground located just a few steps away.

EXTEND THE TRIP

Mamaste Cafe and Play is conveniently located just a one-minute drive from the playground. You can enjoy coffee, pick up a quick snack, or have lunch here. In addition to their café, they offer an admission-based play area designed for young children, aged 5 and under (socks required). If you have older kids with you, they can have fun playing board games or building with Legos outside the supervised area, at no cost.

Mamaste Cafe and Play
1235 Hilton Parma Corners Rd, Hilton, NY 14468

53

55 HUBBELL RD, SPENCERPORT, NY 14559

ALPINE ADVENTURE ZONE

SUMMARY

This playground is massive! For the little ones, there are baby swings and a bench swing. The younger children also enjoy the tunnels, cabin, and smaller balance beams with some assistance. The older kids can often be found playing hide and seek or a game of "The Floor is Lava" after they've finished scaling the bridges and balance beams.

EXTEND THE TRIP

Take a 2-minute drive to Springdale Farm! Visit during the warmer months to see goats, pigs, turkeys, and other farm animals. There's even a robotic milking center here where you can witness cows being milked! If you continue walking past the pond, you can take a short stroll through the woods. Don't forget to bring some cash for donations!

Springdale Farm
700 Colby St, Spencerport, NY 14559

PLAYGROUND DETAILS

Condition: Good

Surface: Mulch

Shade: Playground in direct sun, some shaded spots nearby

Sand Play: No

Water Play: No

Picnic: Limited picnic tables and grills

Creeks/Lakes: None

Wheel Friendly Features: None

Cost: Free

SWINGS
Regular: 4
Adaptive: 0
Baby: 2
Tire: 0
Tandem: 0

8000 W RIDGE RD, BROCKPORT, NY 14420

CLARKSON RECREATION PARK

PLAYGROUND DETAILS

Condition: Good

Surface: Mulch

Shade: None

Sand Play: No

Water Play: No

Picnic: Limited picnic tables available when pavilion not in use

Creeks/Lakes: None

Wheel Friendly Features: Accessible Bankshot™ court

Cost: Free

SWINGS
Regular: 0
Adaptive: 0
Baby: 0
Tire: 0
Tandem: 0

SUMMARY

This is such a fun jungle theme playground! Though there are no swings at this park, there is plenty to entertain. This playground is perfect for climbers and mini thrill seekers with several slides, tunnels and climbing structures. Look for the treasure hunt spinner and find the hidden symbols throughout the playground!

EXTEND THE TRIP

Bring a basketball and play Bankshot™
To Play: "A Bankshot™ player goes from one station to the next. At each station, you bank shots off the bankboards™ and through the nets...

Blue Circle = 2 points
Yellow Circle = 3 points
Red Circle = 5 points

10 points maximum at each station with bonus points awarded at double hoop stations... You try two shots from each circle to make one. If the first try is successful, move on to the next shooting position. You must complete all three circles at each station before moving on to the next station." –BankShot.com

Bankshot™ Court at Kimball Park

56 BARRY ST, BROCKPORT, NY 14420

BARRY STREET PARK

SUMMARY

The playground at Barry Street Park features several slides, a climb-on tunnel, and various balancing structures. However, the highlight of this playground is the zip line with an adaptive seat option! The playground is entirely fenced in, except for a small opening in the back and a wider entrance near the parking lot.

PLAYGROUND DETAILS

Condition: Fair

Surface: Mulch

Shade: None

Sand Play: No

Water Play: No

Picnic: Limited picnic tables

Creeks/Lakes: None

Wheel Friendly Features: Sidewalk cuts through park, ADA picnic table and outhouse

Cost: Free

SWINGS
Regular: 4
Adaptive: 0
Baby: 2
Tire: 0
Tandem: 0

EXTEND THE TRIP

The Village of Brockport is just a 2-minute drive away from the playground, and you can also reach it with a 10-minute walk along sidewalks. In the village, you'll find a variety of options to fill your day, such as shopping at Lift Bridge Book Shop, grabbing a cup of coffee at Java Junction, or strolling along the Erie Canal Heritage Trail.

Village of Brockport
45 Main St, Brockport, NY 14420

4745 REDMAN RD, BROCKPORT, NY 14420

SWEDEN TOWN PARK

PLAYGROUND DETAILS

Condition: Excellent

Surface: Rubber (playground) and cement (splash pad)

Shade: Playground and splash pad in direct sun, large pavilion nearby for shade

Sand Play: No

Water Play: Splash pad

Picnic: Pavilion with picnic tables

Creeks/Lakes: None

Wheel Friendly Features: Zero grade entry to rubber surface, ramps up play structure, zero grade entry merry go round

Cost: Free

SWINGS
The featured playground does not have swings, but other playgrounds within the park do.

SUMMARY

Sweden Town Park offers a great spot to visit on a hot summer day. The largest playground in the park is equipped with musical instruments scattered throughout, a roller slide, and a rubber surface. Adjacent to the playground, you'll find a unique splash pad with moving parts and dumping buckets. This playground and splash pad combo is sure to entertain and is located toward the back of the park.

EXTEND THE TRIP

Pinkies Ice Cream is just a 2-minute drive away from Sweden Town Park! They offer Kiddie Cones for $0.75, making it the perfect post-playground treat. Additionally, they have dairy-free options available. Please note that Pinkies is open seasonally and accepts cash only.

Pinkies Ice Cream
West & Redman Rd, Clarkson, NY 14420

57

1658 LAKE RD N, HAMLIN, NY 14464

HAMLIN RECREATION CENTER

SUMMARY

Adjacent to the recreation center building and directly behind Hamlin's Library, you'll find a majestic wooden playground. The playground is extensive and offers entertainment for kids of all ages. It features baby swings, a tire swing, ample climbing opportunities, hide-and-seek spots, and plenty of space to run around. You'll also discover a unique moving staircase here!

PLAYGROUND DETAILS

Condition: Good

Surface: Mulch

Shade: None

Sand Play: No

Water Play: No

Picnic: Limited benches at playground, pavilion with picnic tables a short walk away

Creeks/Lakes: None

Wheel Friendly Features: None

Cost: Free

EXTEND THE TRIP

The Hamlin Library is just a short walk from the playground, providing a convenient place to relax, cool off, and enjoy some quiet play. While the children's area is small, there are fun activities like a train table and farm animals. You can also access the library's bathrooms during their open hours.

Hamlin Public Library
1680 Lake Rd N, Hamlin, NY 14464

SWINGS
Regular: 2
Adaptive: 0
Baby: 4
Tire: 3
Tandem: 0

58

1420 COUNTY LINE RD, KENDALL, NY 14476
PARTYKA FARMS

PLAYGROUND DETAILS

Condition: Good

Surface: Grass and mulch

Shade: Partial, pavilion and indoor market also available

Sand Play: No

Water Play: No

Picnic: Picnic tables and pavilion outside, food available for purchase inside

Creeks/Lakes: None

Wheel Friendly Features: Various activities such as viewing the goats and exploring play yard elements are located on flat grassy ground.

Cost: Free to play in play yard

SWINGS
Regular: 0
Adaptive: 0
Baby: 0
Tire: 0
Tandem: 0

SUMMARY

Partyka Farms offers a play yard that is free to enter and provides a variety of climbing options, tunnels, goats, tetherball, and cornhole near the playground. The playground features several slides and a tall bridge to cross. This play area is open 7 days a week during the Spring through Fall. Bathrooms can be found inside the market when it's open.

EXTEND THE TRIP

After playing, head inside to shop local products and produce or grab a bite to eat. Here you can buy fresh fruits and vegetables along with many products perfect for gifting. When in season, several varieties of mix and match apples are available to pick from the bins. The ice cream bar at Partyka Farms serves hard and soft ice cream and is available starting in April through mid-October. Visit on Saturdays and Sundays in October for a hayride to their pumpkin patch to pick your own pumpkin!

Inside the market at Partyka Farms

59

1 HAMLIN BEACH STATE PARK, HAMLIN, NY 14464

HAMLIN BEACH STATE PARK

SUMMARY

Area 3 of Hamlin Beach State Park features a playground and a nearby swimming area, making it a great spot for family fun. The playground is just a short walk from the beach, concession stand, and bathhouse. It offers multiple slides, unique bucket swings for little ones, and two-tier tunnels for kids to enjoy. You'll also find several picnic tables and grills nearby, making it a convenient spot for a picnic lunch.

PLAYGROUND DETAILS

Condition: Good

Surface: Mulch

Shade: Playground in direct sun, nearby picnic tables in shade

Sand Play: Yes

Water Play: Swimming beach nearby

Picnic: Picnic tables and grills near playground, concession stand with limited hours also nearby

Creeks/Lakes: The playground is steps away from swimming beach at Lake Ontario

Wheel Friendly Features: Modi mats located in area 3 swimming area for accessibility to the beach,

Cost: Seasonal vehicle entry fee

EXTEND THE TRIP

After some playtime at the playground, a visit to the beach is a must, and your kids probably won't want to leave. If you're looking to extend the trip and enjoy more activities, you can bring your own bean bags to play cornhole just east of the concession stand. It's a great way to have some extra fun at Hamlin Beach State Park.

Area 3 swimming area at Hamlin Beach State Park

SWINGS
Regular: 4
Adaptive: 0
Baby: 2
Tire: 0
Tandem: 0

60

MORRISON RD, LYNDONVILLE, NY 14098

YATES TOWN PARK

PLAYGROUND DETAILS

Condition: Excellent

Surface: Rubber

Shade: Playground in direct sun

Sand Play: No

Water Play: No

Picnic: Pavilion with picnic tables nearby when not in use, picnic tables and grills also scattered throughout park

Creeks/Lakes: Park sits on Lake Ontario

Wheel Friendly Features: Zero grade entry to rubber surface

Cost: Free

SWINGS
Regular: 3
Adaptive: 1
Baby: 1
Tire: 0
Tandem: 0

SUMMARY

This wheel-friendly playground is beautifully situated between wooded areas and Lake Ontario, providing stunning views. It offers play areas suitable for children of all ages and abilities. However, please be aware that the playground is within walking distance of the water, so keep a close watch on your children. Swimming is not allowed in this area.

EXTEND THE TRIP

Finished playing on the playground? Take a moment to appreciate the beautiful surroundings! There's a small pathway encircling the entire playground and pavilion, providing a stroller-friendly walk. Additionally, you'll find a kayak launch and a fishing pier, offering opportunities for extended recreational enjoyment.

MORRISON RD, LYNDONVILLE, NY 14098

BULLARD PARK

SUMMARY

Bullard Park features two playground areas, catering to various age groups, and a lovely splash pad. The wide variety of swings and the wiggling balance beam are particular favorites. Keep in mind that this park is a popular spot for summer parties, so consider visiting on a weekday if you plan to have a picnic under a pavilion.

PLAYGROUND DETAILS

Condition: Good

Surface: Mulch (playground), cement (splash pad)

Shade: Shade from large trees in surrounding green space, pavilions nearby when available

Sand Play: No

Water Play: Splash pad

Picnic: Picnic tables under pavilions when available

Creeks/Lakes: None

Wheel Friendly Features: Accessible splash pad and wheel friendly paths

Cost: Free

EXTEND THE TRIP

Bullard Park offers a loop that circles the entire park, making it ideal for biking, scootering, or taking a stroll with a stroller. The path covers just under 1 mile. Additionally, during the winter, you can visit the park for a fantastic sledding experience on the large hill!

SWINGS
Regular: 6
Adaptive: 0
Baby: 2
Tire: 0
Tandem: 2

PARK AVE, MEDINA, NY 14103
PINE STREET PARK

PLAYGROUND DETAILS

Condition: Good

Surface: Mulch (playground), cement (splash pad)

Shade: None

Sand Play: No

Water Play: Small splash pad

Picnic: Limited picnic tables

Creeks/Lakes: None

Wheel Friendly Features: Zero grade entry paved path leads to water play area

Cost: Free

SWINGS
Regular: 3
Adaptive: 1
Baby: 1
Tire: 0
Tandem: 0

SUMMARY

Pine Street Park is a charming playground located just outside the village of Medina. Children can enjoy a fun sidewalk loop with instructions like "spell your name," "balance," and "twirl" to complete the loop. Additionally, there's a small fountain at the park for water play, providing more entertainment for kids.

EXTEND THE TRIP

A 15-minute walk down the sidewalk or a 2-minute drive will take you to the Medina Railroad Museum. Be sure to check their website for special train ride events or visit from Wednesday to Sunday to explore the largest Railroad and Toy Train Museum in New York State. If you're interested in train excursions, reservations are required. Tickets for the museum can be purchased at the door.

Medina Railroad Museum
530 West Ave, Medina, NY 14103

63

11095 BETHANY CENTER RD, EAST BETHANY, NY 14054

GENESEE COUNTY PARK

SUMMARY

Genesee County Park offers several playgrounds to choose from. While the playgrounds themselves may not be particularly unique, the park is well worth a visit due to the numerous hiking opportunities and areas to explore. With a wide range of amenities, it's an excellent spot for a family gathering. The playground shown is located off of Raymond Road.

EXTEND THE TRIP

Genesee County Park is an expansive park that offers plenty of opportunities for playground hopping and hiking. Don't forget to visit the nature center when it's open. Inside, you'll discover the Discovery Zone, which is filled with hands-on activities for kids. Keep in mind that the road within the park is seasonal, but the nature center remains open year-round.

Genesee County Park Nature Center
11095 Bethany Center Rd, East Bethany, NY 14054

PLAYGROUND DETAILS

Condition: Good

Surface: Mulch

Shade: Partial

Sand Play: No

Water Play: No

Picnic: Pavilion with picnic tables nearby, often in use

Creeks/Lakes: Black Creek runs through the park, but not near playground

Wheel Friendly Features: Nature center is accessible

Cost: Free

SWINGS
Regular: 0
Adaptive: 1
Baby: 1
Tire: 0
Tandem: 0

64

VETERANS MEMORIAL DRIVE, ATTICA, NY 14011

ATTICA MEMORIAL PARK

PLAYGROUND DETAILS

Condition: Good

Surface: Mulch (playground), cement (splash pad)

Shade: Partial

Sand Play: No

Water Play: Splash pad on opposite side of park

Picnic: Several picnic tables and grills nearby, pavilion also nearby

Creeks/Lakes: None

Wheel Friendly Features: Path around park is paved, splash pad and bathroom has zero grade entry

Cost: Free

SWINGS
Regular: 3
Adaptive: 1
Baby: 2
Tire: 1
Tandem: 0

SUMMARY

If you enjoy zip lines, you'll absolutely love Attica Memorial Park! The zip line here comes complete with a ramp for easy access. The rest of the playground offers plenty of entertainment with its woodland-themed tunnels and climbing structures. Be sure to pack a lunch; your visit to this park might last a while!

EXTEND THE TRIP

You can reach the splash pad, located at the opposite end of the park, via the paved path that encircles the park. Enjoy a leisurely stroll with your stroller, wagon, or bikes. The entire circular path is about 1/2 mile long, but it's less than 1/4 mile from the playground to the splash pad.

89 LIBERTY ST, WARSAW, NY 14569

WARSAW VILLAGE PARK

SUMMARY

Whether you prefer swimming in the pool, taking a thrilling ride down the zipline at the playground, or hiking down to view the waterfall, Warsaw Village Park offers something for everyone. It's an ideal destination, especially on a scorching summer day, as it features two pool options: a large wading pool and a lap pool.

PLAYGROUND DETAILS

Condition: Excellent

Surface: Mulch

Shade: Small pavilion

Sand Play: No

Water Play: Two pools adjacent to playground (open July-August) as well as creek nearby

Picnic: Limited picnic tables near playground, alternatively, the village is a short drive or walk away with dining options

Creeks/Lakes: Head up the sledding hill and turn left to find the creek.

Wheel Friendly Features: Small paved path leads to some accessible features

Cost: Free

SWINGS
Regular: 3
Adaptive: 1
Baby: 2
Tire: 0
Tandem: 0

EXTEND THE TRIP

After enjoying the playground and pool, take a walk through the park to discover the creek and waterfall, or if you prefer, you can walk or drive into the village for a delicious meal. Just a 15-minute walk or a quick 2-minute drive from the park, Vertical Cafe awaits, offering a delightful selection of specialty coffee drinks, bubble tea, sandwiches, flatbread pizzas, açaí bowls, and more!

Vertical Cafe
18 W Buffalo St, Warsaw, NY 14569

121 LAKE ST, PERRY, NY 14530

PERRY VILLAGE PARK

PLAYGROUND DETAILS

Condition: Good

Surface: Mulch (playground), cement (splash pad)

Shade: Playground in direct sun, pavilions for shade

Sand Play: No

Water Play: Splash pad

Picnic: Pavilion with several picnic tables nearby

Creeks/Lakes: There is a small pond toward the back of the park, a good distance from the playground

Wheel Friendly Features: Zero grade entry to splash pad

Cost: Free

SWINGS
Regular: 3
Adaptive: 1
Baby: 2
Tire: 0
Tandem: 0

SUMMARY

Perry Village Park indeed offers a unique park experience with its three distinctive playground areas and an exciting splash pad featuring a sea serpent. Children can have a blast exploring the castle-themed play structure and moving between the various play zones. It's a park that promises hours of fun and adventure!

EXTEND THE TRIP

Prehistoric World, just a short 2-minute drive from Perry Village Park, is a fantastic destination for children and families to interact with exotic reptiles and amphibians from around the world. Remember to make reservations in advance through their website to ensure a memorable and educational experience!

Prehistoric World
14 Lake St, Perry, NY 14530

OCTAGON RD GENESEE FALLS, NY 14846
LETCHWORTH: LOWER FALLS

SUMMARY

This playground is a hidden gem within Letchworth State Park, featuring play areas for different age groups and ample shade. To find it, use the "Trail 1 Gorge Lower Falls Trailhead" in your GPS. Keep in mind that you might have limited cell service within the park, so it's best to map out your route before heading out.

PLAYGROUND DETAILS

Condition: Good

Surface: Mulch

Shade: Partial

Sand Play: No

Water Play: No

Picnic: Several picnic tables and grills available and seasonal concession stands throughout park

Creeks/Lakes: Genesee River and the overlooks of the gorge are a short walk away

Wheel Friendly Features: None

Cost: Seasonal vehicle entry fee

EXTEND THE TRIP

It is a short walk to the beautiful Lower Falls area from the playground. Follow the signs for the Lower Falls Trail. After descending the stairs, take a sharp left turn for wide-open views, bridges, and a Lower Falls view. From here, you can turn around or continue on! This area is probably the most scenic of all the spots in the park. It is a popular hike and a common photo opportunity!

Lower Falls area

SWINGS
Regular: 2
Adaptive: 2
Baby: 2
Tire: 0
Tandem: 0

68

5766 PARK RD, CASTILE, NY 14427

LETCHWORTH: WOLF CREEK

PLAYGROUND DETAILS

Condition: Good

Surface: Mulch

Shade: None

Sand Play: No

Water Play: No

Picnic: Picnic area across the street and more shaded picnic tables just down the road

Creeks/Lakes: Wolf Creek is just down the road, entering the water is not permitted

Wheel Friendly Features: None

Cost: Seasonal vehicle entry fee

SWINGS
Regular: 3
Adaptive: 1
Baby: 2
Tire: 0
Tandem: 0

SUMMARY

This playground within Letchworth is located across the street from Eddy's Overlook. After taking in the views of the gorge, head to this playground where the highlight is the massive spider web suspended high off the ground.

EXTEND THE TRIP

Visit the Wolf Creek area for extended scenic views. There is a rough trail that leads from Eddy's Overlook to Wolf Creek. It's a 4-minute walk with a lot of elevation changes, or you can take a quick 1-minute drive west down Park Road. Once at Wolf Creek, you'll find a picturesque setting for a picnic as well as further hiking opportunities along the gorge (best for the older kids!).

Wolf Creek Scenic Waterfalls
5819 Park Rd Castile, New York

69

2244 PARK RD, LEICESTER, NY 14510

LETCHWORTH: HIGHBANKS AREA PLAYGROUND

SUMMARY

The playground on the Mount Morris side of Letchworth is quite amazing. It features a hot air balloon theme with play structures for varying age groups. There are slides of varying heights and swings for various abilities. You are sure to love this playground!

EXTEND THE TRIP

Aside from the vehicle entry fee to get into the park, the Harvey swimming pool is free to enter. Note, this pool is best to visit on very hot days as the water can be very chilly! The pool is open from late June through Labor Day and is located just across the parking lot from Highbanks Area Playground.

Harvey Swimming Pool

PLAYGROUND DETAILS

Condition: New, built in 2022

Surface: Mulch

Shade: Partial

Sand Play: No

Water Play: Harvey Pool on opposite side of parking lot

Picnic: Limited picnic tables near playground but many picnic spots throughout the park

Creeks/Lakes: Take a drive through the park to view the Genesee River and the overlooks of the gorge

Wheel Friendly Features: There is a wide sidewalk that loops around the perimeter of the playground and a ramp on one of the structures

Cost: Seasonal vehicle entry fee

SWINGS
Regular: 6
Adaptive: 2
Baby: 2
Tire: 0
Tandem: 1

70

6103 VISITOR CENTER RD, MT MORRIS, NY 14510

MOUNT MORRIS DAM

PLAYGROUND DETAILS

Condition: Excellent

Surface: Rubber mulch

Shade: None

Sand Play: No

Water Play: No

Picnic: Picnic tables and pavilions nearby

Creeks/Lakes: Views of the gorge and Genesee River steps away from the playground

Wheel Friendly Features: Visitor Center is accessible

Cost: Free

SWINGS
Regular: 0
Adaptive: 0
Baby: 0
Tire: 0
Tandem: 0

SUMMARY

The playground at the Mount Morris Dam has a castle theme, making room for a lot of imaginative play! There are two separate playgrounds here for various age groups. The playground makes for a nice stop before entering the Visitor Center.

EXTEND THE TRIP

After playing on the playground, head inside the Visitor Center to learn more about the dam or to sign up for a free ranger-guided walking tour. While inside the Visitor Center, ask about the scavenger hunt for kids. Once completed, they can pick out a prize!

View of the Dam from the overlook near the playground

71

1 AL LORENZ DR, MT MORRIS, NY 14510

AL LORENZ PARK

SUMMARY

This hidden gem is tucked away in Mount Morris, just outside of Letchworth State Park. Al Lorenz Park boasts a large wooden playground with year-round restrooms. There are different structures for various age groups here and plenty of surrounding green space for further exploration.

EXTEND THE TRIP

You can walk down the hill from the playground to take a stroll around the pond. This is a catch and release pond that is well stocked! There are several bridges here that will bring you to a little island and a path that leads all the way around the pond. Note, if you veer off the trail, be aware of the cliff's edge at the perimeter of the park.

PLAYGROUND DETAILS

Condition: Great, very well maintained.

Surface: Mulch

Shade: Partial

Sand Play: No

Water Play: No

Picnic: Pavilion with picnic tables nearby

Creeks/Lakes: There are ponds within walking distance and the Genesee River gorge borders the park

Wheel Friendly Features: None

Cost: Free

SWINGS
Regular: 2
Adaptive: 0
Baby: 2
Tire: 0
Tandem: 0

350 SPRING ST, AVON, NY 14414

AVON DRIVING PARK

PLAYGROUND DETAILS

Condition: Good

Surface: Mulch

Shade: Some shade in surrounding green space

Sand Play: No

Water Play: No

Picnic: Bring a blanket to picnic under the shade of a tree, pavilion also available a short walk away

Creeks/Lakes: Creek access along trail

Wheel Friendly Features: None

Cost: Free

SWINGS
Regular: 8
Adaptive: 1
Baby: 3
Tire: 0
Tandem: 0

SUMMARY

There are two wooden play structures here – one appropriate for younger kids and one better suited for kids 5-12. There is also a merry-go-round as well as an adaptive swing, baby swings, and typical swings. The kids will love to climb through the tunnel, up the rock wall, and dig in the rocks.

EXTEND THE TRIP

Within the park, you'll discover a scenic walking trail that guides you to a charming creek area. Take caution, as the water can become deep, so keep a watchful eye. To locate this picturesque spot, your best starting point is the parking lot nearest to the playground and track. From there, head southward in the direction of the fitness trail. As you progress, you'll notice a mowed path leading into the woods. Continue along the trail until you come across a rough path that leads to the creek. It is less than 1/2 mile to the creek area.

Concuss Creek, Avon Driving Park

7384 ZIEGLER DR, LIMA, NY 14485

MARK TUBBS PARK

SUMMARY

Mark Tubbs Park features both a wooden playground and a standard play structure. The playground is partially shaded and offers slides for children of all ages. Don't forget to bring your bikes! There's a paved path that loops around the park, which is just under 1/2 mile long. It's a great place for kids to practice their bike-riding skills!

PLAYGROUND DETAILS

Condition: Fair

Surface: Mulch

Shade: Partial

Sand Play: No

Water Play: No

Picnic: There's limited picnic tables a short walk from the playground as well as a grill

Creeks/Lakes: None

Wheel Friendly Features: Paved path that loops around the park

Cost: Free

SWINGS
Regular: 0
Adaptive: 1
Baby: 1
Tire: 0
Tandem: 0

EXTEND THE TRIP

Milk & Honey Cafe is situated in the heart of the Village of Lima and is only a 3-minute drive from Mark Tubbs Park. This cafe offers a cozy atmosphere with indoor and outdoor seating options, a variety of bakery items, and specialty coffee drinks. It's a great place to relax and grab a bite to eat after your visit to the park!

Milk & Honey Cafe
7294 W Main St, Lima, NY 14485

74

JACK EVANS DR. HONEOYE, NEW YORK 14471

SANDY BOTTOM PARK

PLAYGROUND DETAILS

Condition: Good

Surface: Mulch

Shade: Partial

Sand Play: Beach nearby

Water Play: Beach nearby

Picnic: Limited picnic tables near playground, pavilion with picnic tables towards back of park

Creeks/Lakes: This park sits on Honeoye Lake

Wheel Friendly Features: The trail from the beach to the village is wheel friendly

Cost: Free

SWINGS
Regular: 2
Adaptive: 0
Baby: 2
Tire: 0
Tandem: 0

SUMMARY

Sandy Bottom Park provides a wonderful lakeside experience on Honeoye Lake. The park features two charming playgrounds located close to the beach, offering a pleasant mix of sun and shade. While the playgrounds are at a safe distance from the water, they're conveniently situated for easy access. The beach is open when lifeguards are on duty.

EXTEND THE TRIP

For a delightful post-beach experience, follow the trail from Sandy Bottom Park to Birdhouse Brewing. This scenic trail covers just under half a mile one way and features a flat, stroller-friendly gravel path. At Birdhouse Brewing, you can savor delicious food and drinks, and you might also find a market offering local products at different times of the year. During the summer season, you can enjoy outdoor concerts at the brewery. Additionally, explore the nearby shops for more local items and treasures.

Birdhouse Brewing
8716 Main St, Honeoye, NY 14471

6472 GULICK RD, NAPLES, NY 14512

RMSC CUMMING NATURE CENTER

SUMMARY

Cumming Nature Center in Naples is a hidden gem that's well worth the drive. This environmental education center offers unique trails and features a natural playground. The playground is a delightful introduction to the beautiful pine forest and can be found at the start of the yellow trail, towards the back of the courtyard. It includes a small hut, a log balance beam, and several other stump and log structures for climbing.

PLAYGROUND DETAILS

Condition: Fair

Surface: Stone/dirt

Shade: Yes

Sand Play: No

Water Play: No

Picnic: Plenty of green space for a picnic blanket as well as a pavilion with picnic tables

Creeks/Lakes: Several creeks and ponds throughout the park, but not near the playground

Wheel Friendly Features: The nature center and several trails are wheel friendly

Cost: The Nature Center is free for RMSC members and CNC Pine Pass members, $3 per person/$10 per family for the general public and $5 per person/$15 per family during skiing & snowshoeing season

SWINGS
Regular: 0
Adaptive: 0
Baby: 0
Tire: 0
Tandem: 0

EXTEND THE TRIP

In addition to hiking the trails and enjoying the playground, make sure to visit the discovery room downstairs at Cumming Nature Center. The discovery room offers various activities, including a touch table, craft station, animal bins with different furs and footprints to explore, and stations to match animals with their category and habitat. Make sure to check the opening hours before heading out!

Inside RMSC Cumming Nature Center

6475 GANNETT HILL PARK DR, NAPLES, NY 14512

ONTARIO COUNTY PARK

PLAYGROUND DETAILS

Condition: Good

Surface: Mulch

Shade: Playground in direct sun, nearby pavilion for shade

Sand Play: No

Water Play: No

Picnic: Pavilion with picnic tables nearby

Creeks/Lakes: None

Wheel Friendly Features: ADA trail within park

Cost: Free

SWINGS
Regular: 4
Adaptive: 0
Baby: 0
Tire: 0
Tandem: 0

SUMMARY

The first playground you'll encounter at Ontario County Park is meant for campers, but continue on and you'll find a parking area for the bigger playground. This playground has several slides and big artificial rocks to climb on. Nearby, there are wide open fields that often have a nice breeze, making it a great spot for flying a kite and enjoying the stunning views!

EXTEND THE TRIP

Explore the hiking trails for some breathtaking views. There are numerous trails and pathways available. Some of these trails are suitable for strollers and wheelchairs, while others are not, so consider bringing a baby carrier if you plan to venture deeper into the woods with little ones. The Finger Lakes trail, in particular, features an ADA-approved path with an accessible overlook. Beyond this point, the trails wind through hilly terrain. As this location boasts high elevation, be mindful of some steep slopes. It's advisable to hold hands and keep a close watch!

ADA Lookout Trail
Ontario County Park

4965 CO RD 16, CANANDAIGUA, NY 14424

ONANDA PARK

SUMMARY

Onanda Park features a well-maintained playground located next to a picturesque beach on Canandaigua Lake. The playground offers a variety of play structures, including large tunnels, slides of varying lengths, pull-up bars, and a shapes/colors board. It's designed to accommodate a wide age range with two separate structures for different age groups.

EXTEND THE TRIP

Visiting Onanda Park wouldn't be complete without spending some time at the beach. While the beach surface is covered with rocks rather than sand, you can still bring a shovel and bucket for some fun play. The beach area is usually open until Labor Day, and you can check the town's website for schedule information. Additionally, consider exploring the hiking trails to see the waterfall for an added adventure.

Onanada Park Beach

PLAYGROUND DETAILS

Condition: Good

Surface: Mulch

Shade: Shade can be found in surrounding green space

Sand Play: No

Water Play: Beach and creek nearby

Picnic: Limited picnic tables scattered throughout park

Creeks/Lakes: This park sites on Canandaigua Lake

Wheel Friendly Features: None

Cost: You can purchase season ($35), weekday ($5), and weekend/holiday ($7) passes per vehicle. Walk in passes ($1) also available

SWINGS
Regular: 0
Adaptive: 0
Baby: 0
Tire: 0
Tandem: 0

155 LAKESHORE DR, CANANDAIGUA, NY 14424

KERSHAW PARK

PLAYGROUND DETAILS

Condition: Good

Surface: Mulch

Shade: None

Sand Play: Beach access nearby (with admission fee)

Water Play: Beach access nearby (with admission fee)

Picnic: Pavilions, grills and picnic tables nearby

Creeks/Lakes: Playground sits right on Canandaigua Lake

Wheel Friendly Features: Paved path through park

Cost: Free

SWINGS
Regular: 0
Adaptive: 0
Baby: 0
Tire: 0
Tandem: 0

SUMMARY

Kershaw Park is a beautiful area situated right on Canandaigua Lake. It features a charming playground that benefits from a refreshing breeze from the lake. Children can have a great time climbing on the frog and turtle play structures and sliding down the slides. There are pathways for leisurely strolls along the lake, and you can find seasonal restrooms in the bath house when it's open.

EXTEND THE TRIP

If you're visiting on a hot day, you can cool off by stopping by the nearby Kershaw Beach, where entry fees apply. Enjoy a refreshing dip in the lake and relax on the sandy beach. Alternatively, you can take a short 5-minute walk to Scoops Ice Cream to enjoy some sweet treats to beat the heat!

Scoops Ice Cream
10 Lakeshore Dr, Canandaigua, NY 14424

185 BUFFALO ST, CANANDAIGUA, NY 14424

FRANK BAKER PARK

SUMMARY

Frank Baker Park features an enjoyable playground with swings and various climbing and balance structures suitable for older kids. In addition to the playground, the park offers soccer fields, tennis courts, seasonal bathrooms, and a story walk. The story walk path is suitable for strollers, bikes, and scooters and forms a loop that is approximately 1/3 mile in length.

PLAYGROUND DETAILS

Condition: Good

Surface: Mulch

Shade: None

Sand Play: No

Water Play: No

Picnic: Picnic tables and pavilion available when not in use

Creeks/Lakes: None

Wheel Friendly Features: Story trail is wheel friendly

Cost: Free

EXTEND THE TRIP

The Wood Library is conveniently located just a 4-minute drive from Frank Baker Park. It features a spacious children's section with a dedicated area for imaginative play. Kids will enjoy exploring various themed rooms, a puppet theater, and a train table for hours of creative fun! The Wood Library is part of the OWWL Library System, providing a wide range of resources for residents and visitors.

Wood Library
134 N Main St, Canandaigua, NY 14424

SWINGS
Regular: 4
Adaptive: 0
Baby: 4
Tire: 0
Tandem: 0

2550 OUTHOUSE RD, CANANDAIGUA, NY 14424

RICHARD P. OUTHOUSE MEMORIAL PARK

PLAYGROUND DETAILS

Condition: Good

Surface: Rubber mulch

Shade: None

Sand Play: No

Water Play: No

Picnic: Pavilion with picnic tables nearby

Creeks/Lakes: None

Wheel Friendly Features: Wide paved trail around park

Cost: Free

SWINGS
Regular: 4
Adaptive: 0
Baby: 2
Tire: 0
Tandem: 0

SUMMARY

Richard P Outhouse Memorial Park playground is well-loved for its pirate ship theme. After navigating the ships, kids can stop and explore the dinosaur egg and dinosaur bone structures. This is a sunny playground, so don't forget to pack your shades!

EXTEND THE TRIP

Pack the bikes, scooters, or roller blades! There is a beautifully paved path around the park that passes by the playground, fitness court, and basketball court. It can also be used to access Motion Junction on the other side of the park. Just use caution when crossing the road!

Richard P. Outhouse Memorial Park Fitness Track

2640 OUTHOUSE RD, CANANDAIGUA, NY 14424
MOTION JUNCTION INCLUSIVE PLAYGROUND

SUMMARY

Motion Junction at Richard P. Outhouse Park West is a universal playground that's fully inclusive. It features equipment designed to promote parallel play opportunities, including a 3-bay 50-foot zip line with various seating options. This playground is universally designed, creating a seamless environment for all children to play alongside their peers, siblings, parents, and grandparents.

EXTEND THE TRIP

Canandaigua offers a multitude of play opportunities. You can walk, drive, or wheel over to the second playground at Richard P. Outhouse Park (see page 81). Alternatively, take a 5-minute drive to the village of Canandaigua, where you'll find kid-friendly favorites like Mightea Boba and the neighboring Unique Toy Shop.

MighTea Boba & Unique Toy Shop
116 S Main St, Canandaigua, NY 14424

PLAYGROUND DETAILS

Condition: Excellent

Surface: Rubber

Shade: Playground in direct sun, nearby pavilion for shade

Sand Play: No

Water Play: No

Picnic: Picnic tables under pavilion

Creeks/Lakes: None

Wheel Friendly Features: The playground is fully accessible

Cost: Free

SWINGS
Regular: 2
Adaptive: 4
Baby: 2
Tire: 1
Tandem: 1

7405 DRYER RD, VICTOR, NY 14564

DRYER ROAD PARK

PLAYGROUND DETAILS

Condition: Fair

Surface: Mulch

Shade: None

Sand Play: No

Water Play: No

Picnic: Pavilion with picnic tables nearby

Creeks/Lakes: None

Wheel Friendly Features: None (except for the bike-friendly trails)

Cost: Free

SWINGS
Regular: 2
Adaptive: 0
Baby: 2
Tire: 0
Tandem: 0

SUMMARY

The main attraction at Dryer Road Park is the large mountain bike skills area and trails within the park. While this area was not designed for young children, it can be fun to explore when not in use. When it is in use, it can be entertaining to watch the experts before heading to the playground. The playground has two structures for different age groups.

EXTEND THE TRIP

Take a 5-minute drive to enjoy a cone at nearby Papa Jack's Ice Cream Shop and stroll through the Village of Victor. Papa Jack's Ice Cream offers dairy-free and gluten-free options. Please note that this establishment accepts cash only!

Papa Jack's Ice Cream
265 W Main St, Victor, NY 14564

83

6680 PAPARONE DR, VICTOR, NY 14564

VICTOR MUNICIPAL PARK

SUMMARY

Victor Municipal Park is tucked away from the street, offering a less crowded and peaceful atmosphere. The park provides opportunities for fishing, hiking, and ample space for running around. The fairly large playground features multiple tunnels, a climbing slide, and numerous monkey bars for kids to enjoy. Don't forget to explore the story trail after playing!

PLAYGROUND DETAILS

Condition: Good

Surface: Mulch

Shade: Playground in direct sun, some shade in surrounding green space and pavilion

Sand Play: No

Water Play: No

Picnic: Limited picnic tables near playground

Creeks/Lakes: None

Wheel Friendly Features: None

Cost: Free

SWINGS
Regular: 2
Adaptive: 1
Baby: 1
Tire: 1
Tandem: 0

EXTEND THE TRIP

Busy Bean Cafe is a kid-friendly cafe located in the village of Victor. Whether you visit the cafe directly or make it a part of your stroll from Victor Municipal Park, it's a great spot for families. The cafe offers a cozy kid's section equipped with toys and books. You can reach the cafe with a quick 5-minute drive from the park, or take a leisurely 15-minute stroll (or a quicker bike ride) by following the Trolley Trail.

Busy Bean Cafe
10 E Main St #106, Victor, NY 14564

1394 MERTENSIA RD, FARMINGTON, NY 14425

MERTENSIA PARK

PLAYGROUND DETAILS

Condition: New, built in 2023

Surface: Rubber mulch

Shade: None

Sand Play: No

Water Play: No

Picnic: Limited picnic tables

Creeks/Lakes: Mud Creek runs along walking path

Wheel Friendly Features: None

Cost: Free

SWINGS
Regular: 2
Adaptive: 1
Baby: 1
Tire: 0
Tandem: 0

SUMMARY

The newly built playground at Mertensia Park may be on the smaller side, but it offers some unique features to keep kids entertained. These include mini monkey bars, a rope bridge, and a magic answer wheel. Additionally, there's a swing set and large boulders near the playground that kids often enjoy.

EXTEND THE TRIP

After some playtime at the playground, you can explore the nearby creek area. To access the creek, take a short walk from the trailhead (look for the blue sign located near the basketball courts and follow the trail into the woods). There, you'll have the opportunity to explore the creek bed and follow the trail to the lodge or loop back to the starting point. However, it's important to note that there is a lot of poison ivy along the trail near the creek. Additionally, the water in the creek can be deep and fast-moving, so it's not suitable for a creek walk or wading.

Mud Creek along Rotary Centennial Walking Path at Mertensia Park

1000 CO RD 8, FARMINGTON, NY 14425

FARMINGTON TOWN PARK

SUMMARY

At Farmington Town Park, you'll discover two sandboxes. One of these sandboxes is at ground level and includes a digger for play, while the other sandbox is raised off the ground to ensure wheelchair accessibility. In addition to these sandboxes, the park offers various play features, such as a balance beam, swings, slides, and a story trail. Please note that dogs are not allowed at this park.

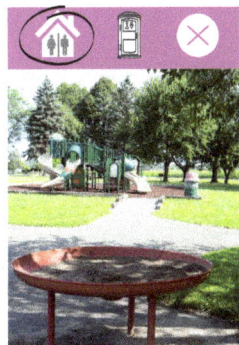

PLAYGROUND DETAILS

Condition: Excellent

Surface: Rubber mulch

Shade: Playground in direct sun, shade in surrounding green space

Sand Play: Yes

Water Play: No

Picnic: Limited picnic tables near playground

Creeks/Lakes: None

Wheel Friendly Features: Paved path leads to accessible sand box

Cost: Free

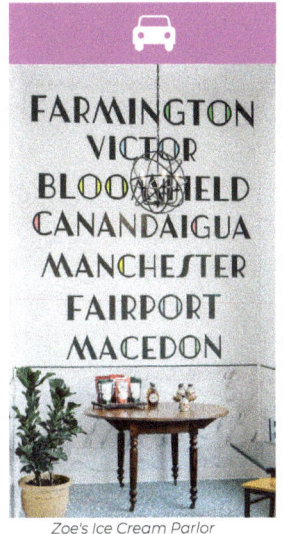

SWINGS
Regular: 2
Adaptive: 1
Baby: 2
Tire: 0
Tandem: 0

EXTEND THE TRIP

Farmington Town Park is just a short drive away from the lively area of Farmington, offering a variety of dining options. If you're looking to cool down after your visit to the playground on a hot summer day, consider stopping by Zoe's Ice Cream Parlor. Zoe's serves Perry's and Gifford's ice cream, as well as gelato. It's open year round and provides an allergy chart at the register for those with dietary restrictions. Enjoy a sweet treat after your park adventure!

Zoe's Ice Cream Parlor
1270 Commercial Dr, Farmington, NY 14425

LORRAINE DR, WALWORTH, NY 14568

GINEGAW PARK

PLAYGROUND DETAILS

Condition: Good

Surface: Mulch

Shade: Partial

Sand Play: Yes, sandbox with digger

Water Play: No

Picnic: Pavilion with picnic tables and grill available when not in use, plenty of green space in the shade for a picnic blanket

Creeks/Lakes: None

Wheel Friendly Features: None

Cost: Free

SWINGS
Regular: 3
Adaptive: 1
Baby: 2
Tire: 0
Tandem: 1

SUMMARY

Ginegaw Park offers a range of fun features for kids and parents to enjoy. The playground includes a "mommy and me" swing, sandbox with a digger, stand-up teeter-totter, and barrel tunnels. Additionally, you'll find some nostalgic pieces such as two metal slides and spring riders. While there is a seasonal bathroom shelter within the park, it's worth noting that it's a bit of a walk (or a short drive) from the playground.

EXTEND THE TRIP

For a small space, the Walworth-Seely Public Library packs a strong children's section. This library is just a 1-minute drive from the Ginegaw Park playground. While it's open to everyone, it's worth noting that this library is part of the OWWL Library System. As a result, residents of Ontario, Wayne, Wyoming, and Livingston counties can borrow materials with a valid library card.

Walworth-Seely Public Library
3600 Lorraine Dr, Walworth, NY 14568

4072 PARK AVE, MARION, NY 14505

MARION TOWN PARK

SUMMARY

This is a unique playground designed primarily for toddlers and preschoolers. Children will enjoy the wide selection of swings, musical play elements, and climbing structures. If you're visiting with a little one, don't forget to try the tandem swing!

PLAYGROUND DETAILS

Condition: Good

Surface: Mulch

Shade: Playground in direct sun, pavilion nearby

Sand Play: No

Water Play: No

Picnic: Pavilion with picnic tables

Creeks/Lakes: None

Wheel Friendly Features: None

Cost: Free

EXTEND THE TRIP

Lollypops & Polkadots is a children's clothing store (with used and new items) located just 2 minutes from the park. This local business is adorable! You are sure to find something for your kids here and at a great price!

Lollypops & Polkadots
3793 S Main St, Marion, NY 14505

SWINGS
Regular: 2
Adaptive: 0
Baby: 2
Tire: 0
Tandem: 2

88

6551 KNICKERBOCKER RD, ONTARIO, NY 14519

CASEY PARK

PLAYGROUND DETAILS

Condition: Good

Surface: Mulch

Shade: Playground in direct sun, nearby pavilion for shade

Sand Play: Coarse sand in beach area when open

Water Play: Beach and splash pad, call ahead to ensure beach is open and splash pad is running

Picnic: Pavilion with picnic tables near playground

Creeks/Lakes: Pond nearby with swimming area when lifeguard is on duty

Wheel Friendly Features: None

Cost: Free

SWINGS
Regular: 2
Adaptive: 1
Baby: 2
Tire: 0
Tandem: 0

SUMMARY

This park is filled with fun opportunities for the whole family. There are two modern playgrounds here, Just a couple paces from the first playground is a larger playground housing the highest three story tunnel slide around, lookout windows, rainbow slide and a massive rock wall. Geared for older kids, your pre-teens will even love this one!

EXTEND THE TRIP

Beyond the two playgrounds, splash pad and beach, you can extend the trip further by taking a walk. The stroller friendly path starts behind the playground with a story walk and winds through the woods. If you venture far enough, you will find a bird watching shelter!

Bird watching shelter at Casey Park

89

4507 LAKE RD, WILLIAMSON, NY 14589

B. FOREMAN PARK

SUMMARY

B. Foreman Park is a beautiful waterfront park with strong historic connections and multiple playgrounds. It is a great location for a shaded picnic or a sunset walk. The playground is small but has a lot of play potential. There's even a story trail often on display along the perimeter of the playground. Note that the swings are not near the playground; instead, they are across the parking lot, near the lake.

PLAYGROUND DETAILS

Condition: Excellent

Surface: Mulch

Shade: Playground is in direct sun, shade in surrounding green space

Sand Play: No

Water Play: No

Picnic: Several picnic tables and grills throughout park

Creeks/Lakes: Park sits on Lake Ontario, access to the water is not permitted here

Wheel Friendly Features: None

Cost: Free

SWINGS
Regular: 4
Adaptive: 0
Baby: 2
Tire: 0
Tandem: 0

EXTEND THE TRIP

While in the area, be sure to visit Cornwall Preserve. This park is a 3-minute drive from B. Foreman Park and offers a unique hike with views of Lake Ontario and trails through fields and woods. Although this trail isn't stroller-friendly, it's fairly flat and easy for kids to complete. Please note that Cornwall Preserve is closed on Wednesdays for orchard management.

Cornwall Preserve
53975 Lake Rd, Williamson, NY 14589

7958 WICKHAM BLVD, SODUS POINT, NY 14555

SODUS POINT BEACH PARK

PLAYGROUND DETAILS

Condition: Good

Surface: Sand

Shade: Playground in direct sun, large pavilion nearby for shade

Sand Play: Playground is surrounded by sand

Water Play: Beach with lifeguards

Picnic: Large pavilion with picnic tables as well as concession stand

Creeks/Lakes: Playground on Lake Ontario beach

Wheel Friendly Features: Modi mat for accessibility to the beach

Cost: Free

SWINGS
Regular: 0
Adaptive: 0
Baby: 2
Tire: 0
Tandem: 0

SUMMARY

Conveniently located near the large pavilion and just a few steps from the lake, there's a playground in the sand. Please note that being on the beach, there is little shade, and the equipment can get hot. Don't forget the sunscreen!

For sand play, you can check out the toy library in front of the bath shelter. This is a great place to donate any sand toys you no longer need!

EXTEND THE TRIP

If the on-site concession stand doesn't suit your needs, you can head into town for more dining options. Hots Point is a 3-minute drive from the beach and offers kid-friendly dining. Alternatively, you can explore Burnap's Farm Market, which is a 9-minute drive away. There, you'll find farm animals, a local market, lunch and dinner options, and a large play area that is free to explore.

Hots Point
8482 Greig St, Sodus Point, NY 14555

5 RAILROAD AVE, CLIFTON SPRINGS, NY 14432

JOHN BROWN MEMORIAL PARK

SUMMARY

John Brown Memorial Park has two play spaces: The first is for the little ones with age-appropriate equipment, mulch diggers and a rock wall cave to climb on and into. The second playground has larger equipment, unique basketball hoops and plenty of swings. There is a lot of space to explore as well as a beautiful pavilion to picnic in nearby. Note, there are restrooms at the park but they are not always available.

EXTEND THE TRIP

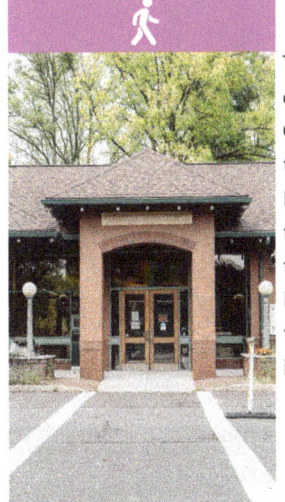

The playground sits just outside the quaint village of Clifton Springs and is across the street from the library. Plan ahead and visit on days the library is open! It is easiest to park in the library parking lot and stroll to the park from there after playing in the inviting children's section.

Clifton Springs Library
4 Railroad Ave, Clifton Springs, NY 14432

PLAYGROUND DETAILS

Condition: Good

Surface: Mulch

Shade: Playground is partially shaded, large pavilion nearby

Sand Play: No

Water Play: No

Picnic: Large pavilion with picnic tables nearby

Creeks/Lakes: Sulphur creek runs behind playground

Wheel Friendly Features: None

Cost: Free

SWINGS
Regular: 3
Adaptive: 0
Baby: 3
Tire: 1
Tandem: 0

309 LAKE ST, PENN YAN, NY 14527

PHELPS COMMUNITY CENTER

PLAYGROUND DETAILS

Condition: Excellent, well kept

Surface: Mulch

Shade: Playground in direct sun

Sand Play: No

Water Play: No

Picnic: 2 wooden picnic tables located next to each playground, plenty of room and shade for a blanket picnic, local dining options within walking distance

Creeks/Lakes: No

Wheel Friendly Features: None

Cost: Free

SWINGS
Regular: 3
Adaptive: 1
Baby: 1
Tire: 0
Tandem: 1

SUMMARY

There are two areas for different ages and abilities at Phelps Community Center. One is an adorable bug themed play area (pictured below). This play area is is completely fenced in with locking gates. The other playground is not fenced in but has some really imaginative and unique equipment (pictured left). Bathrooms are available when the Community Center is open.

EXTEND THE TRIP

There are several options to extend your trip here. Older kids may be interested in checking out the courts and outdoor fitness center near the playground. Alternatively, you can head inside the Community Center to visit the library.
If you prefer to go on a hike before or after your playground visit, a trailhead to the Ontario County Pathway is just a 4-minute drive down the road. This section of the trail features beautiful waterfalls!

Ontario County Pathway, 2011 NY-96, Clifton Springs, NY 14432

93

309 LAKE ST, PENN YAN, NY 14527

RED JACKET PARK

SUMMARY

Located at the top of Keuka Lake, this park offers a beautiful spot to find shade, visit a playground, and cool off in the lake. The big kid structure features monkey bars and several climbing obstacles, as well as an interactive music board and bongos. The toddler structure is simple and unique with an 'ABC' stairway, small stairs, and a miniature slide.

EXTEND THE TRIP

There is a small beach just beyond the playground at Red Jacket Park, perfect for little ones wanting to splash in the water. Swimming is allowed when a lifeguard is on duty.

This park is about an hour's drive from the city of Rochester but makes for a great stop if you're exploring Penn Yan for the day. Consider stopping by Oak Hill Bulk Foods and the Spotted Duck while in the area

Red Jacket Park Beach

PLAYGROUND DETAILS

Condition: Good

Surface: Mulch

Shade: Partial

Sand Play: No

Water Play: Nearby beach

Picnic: Picnic tables and grills throughout park

Creeks/Lakes: Park sits on Keuka Lake

Wheel Friendly Features: None

Cost: Free

SWINGS
Regular: 2
Adaptive: 2
Baby: 1
Tire: 0
Tandem: 0

47 LAKE FRONT DR, GENEVA, NY 14456

GENEVA COMMUNITY LAKEFRONT PLAYGROUND

PLAYGROUND DETAILS

Condition: Good

Surface: Mulch

Shade: None

Sand Play: No

Water Play: No

Picnic: Limited picnic tables at playground, several picnic tables for enjoying ice cream at the nearby ice cream shop

Creeks/Lakes: Playground sits on Seneca Lake

Wheel Friendly Features: Musical instruments and other sensory features located on small rubber surface with zero grade entry

Cost: Free

SWINGS
Regular: 0
Adaptive: 0
Baby: 2
Tire: 1
Tandem: 0

SUMMARY

This beautiful playground is located right off Seneca Lake and a stone's throw away from the Finger Lakes Welcome Center. The playground is modern and imaginative with several different climbing structures, along with baby swings for the littlest ones. There is also an inclusive merry-go-round and some musical features here as well.

EXTEND THE TRIP

Long Pier Ice Cream is right next to the playground. Grab a cone and take a stroll along Seneca Lake. You can even walk to the Finger Lakes Welcome Center from here. See the next page for details.

Long Pier Ice Cream

FINGER LAKES WELCOME CENTER

35 LAKE FRONT DR, GENEVA, NY 14456

SUMMARY

The Finger Lakes Welcome Center's playground is imaginative and nicely padded! The entire area has a ship theme with a "water" image rubber surface and faux rocks and vines for climbing. The playground is mostly fenced in with a simple 2 rail fence and hedges. Bathrooms are located within the Welcome Center when open.

PLAYGROUND DETAILS

Condition: Good

Surface: Rubber

Shade: None

Sand Play: No

Water Play: No

Picnic: Several picnic tables near playground, food for purchase within Welcome Center

Creeks/Lakes: The Welcome Center sits on Seneca Lake

Wheel Friendly Features: Zero grade entry to rubber surface and paved paths along lake

Cost: Free

SWINGS
Regular: 0
Adaptive: 0
Baby: 0
Tire: 0
Tandem: 0

EXTEND THE TRIP

The playground is conveniently located just outside the Welcome Center. Inside the center, you'll find a great place to cool off or warm up, depending on the time of year. If you're looking for a snack or meal, they offer food and beverage options sourced from local farmers and wineries. When you enter the Welcome Center, don't forget to check out the floor, where you'll find a map of the Finger Lakes region. To continue your adventure, explore the story walk outside the Welcome Center and take a leisurely walk along Seneca Lake to reach the Geneva Community Lakefront Playground.

Finger Lakes Welcome Center

96

100 WATERLOO GENEVA RD, GENEVA, NY 13165

SENECA LAKE STATE PARK

PLAYGROUND DETAILS

Condition: Good

Surface: Mulch (playground), cement (splash pad)

Shade: None

Sand Play: Beach with coarse sand nearby

Water Play: Splash pad and beach

Picnic: Several picnic tables and grills throughout park, concession stand near playground

Creeks/Lakes: This park sits on Seneca Lake

Wheel Friendly Features: Paved paths throughout park, accessible splash pad with water safe wheelchairs available

Cost: Seasonal vehicle entry fee

SWINGS
Regular: 0
Adaptive: 0
Baby: 0
Tire: 2
Tandem: 0

SUMMARY

Seneca Lake State Park is an ideal destination for a day trip. The main playground features exciting amenities like a zip-line, a large spinning sphere, a small play area for little ones, and some ride-on spring toys. In close proximity, you'll discover a unique splash pad equipped with 100 water jets. The splash pad operates using recycled water and follows a cycle of being on for 1 hour and off for 20 minutes. Please note that vinyl covers are required for children in swim diapers.

EXTEND THE TRIP

At Seneca Lake State Park, you can enjoy an entire day of fun without needing to drive elsewhere. The park offers three playgrounds within walking distance, along with a beach, a splash pad, and a concession stand. For those looking to explore multiple playgrounds, there are wide paved paths connecting each one, making it a great spot to bring bikes and scooters. Get ready for a day filled with endless play!

Seneca Lake State Park alternative playground

97

6096 NY-96A, ROMULUS, NY 14541

SAMPSON STATE PARK

SUMMARY

While this park may require a bit of a drive for most, it's an absolute must-visit! The playground here offers a definite 'wow' factor. With a several-story slide that's sure to entertain the older kids and a pirate-themed structure equipped with numerous gadgets to amuse the little ones, there's something for everyone. And when you're ready to cool off, don't forget to visit the nearby beach. Keep in mind that the park is open from April through October.

PLAYGROUND DETAILS

Condition: Good

Surface: Mulch

Shade: None

Sand Play: Nearby beach

Water Play: Nearby beach

Picnic: Minimal picnic tables near playground, concession stand short walk away

Creeks/Lakes: The playground is just a few paces away from Seneca Lake

Wheel Friendly Features: None

Cost: Subject to seasonal vehicle entry fee, though not always collected

EXTEND THE TRIP

If the playground and beach aren't enough to fill the day, consider driving over to the Military Museum within the park. Inside, you'll discover a narrative about the hundreds of thousands of sailors and airmen who trained here from 1942 until 1956. Additionally, if you're visiting in the summer, Sampson State Park offers an outdoor theater. Check the show schedule online and enjoy a family-friendly film under the stars.

Sampson State Park Military Museum

SWINGS
Regular: 5
Adaptive: 0
Baby: 4
Tire: 0
Tandem: 0

98

LOWER LAKE RD, LODI, NY 14860

LODI POINT STATE MARINE PARK

PLAYGROUND DETAILS

Condition: Good

Surface: Mulch

Shade: Playground in direct sun

Sand Play: No

Water Play: Seneca Lake is a short walk from the playground for dipping toes in

Picnic: Several picnic tables and grills scattered throughout the park

Creeks/Lakes: The playground sits on Seneca Lake

Wheel Friendly Features: None

Cost: Seasonal vehicle entry fee

SWINGS
Regular: 3
Adaptive: 1
Baby: 2
Tire: 0
Tandem: 0

SUMMARY

Lodi Point State Park is a hidden gem. Despite its small size, it offers a beautiful and entertaining experience for family and friends. The park features two playground areas: one designed for little ones, featuring a boat-shaped structure, and another tailored for older kids, with numerous opportunities for climbing, scaling, and sliding.

EXTEND THE TRIP

Pack some food, grab a picnic table and grill and enjoy the sound of the lake with a meal after playing on the playground. Afterward, be sure to stroll the beach and see what treasures can be found there!

Seaglass found at Lodi Point State Park

COUNTY RD 116, SENECA FALLS, NY 13148

CAYUGA LAKE STATE PARK

SUMMARY

Put this one on the summer bucket list! Cayuga Lake State Park has a very unique playground with a pirate ship theme right along Cayuga Lake! There are multiple playground structures here that are well spaced, as well as some unique swings and baby swings. Want to make a trip out of it? This playground is nearest campsites 1-36 through you do need to cross the road to get to the playground from the campsites.

EXTEND THE TRIP

The lakefront and beach are very close to the playground. It is a very short walk to the bathhouse and beach from the playground, making for a great spot to spend the day. The beach has course sand and the water is shallow for a good distance. Pack the sunscreen and beach toys!

Cayuga Lake State Park Beach

PLAYGROUND DETAILS

Condition: Good

Surface: Mulch

Shade: Playground is in direct sun, some shaded green space nearby

Sand Play: Beach with coarse sand nearby

Water Play: Beach nearby, swim at own risk

Picnic: Picnic tables and grills throughout park

Creeks/Lakes: Playground sits on Cayuga Lake

Wheel Friendly Features: None

Cost: Seasonal vehicle entry fee

SWINGS
Regular: 0
Adaptive: 0
Baby: 0
Tire: 0
Tandem: 0

100

ABOUT THE AUTHOR

Meet Sara Snyder, library/media specialist at her local school and a devoted mother to two wonderful kids, aged 8 and 5. Nestled in the serenity of her small hobby farm, she has nurtured not only her family but also a deep-rooted love for playgrounds and the exploration of Greater Rochester. Sara's enthusiasm for discovering the region's hidden gems extends from the heart of the city to the outskirts of the Finger Lakes.

Her journey to create "Rochester's Playbook: 100 Beloved Playgrounds" was a labor of love, fueled by her desire to share the joy and wonder of these play spaces with others. However, the realization of this comprehensive guide would not have been possible without the unwavering support of her family, the encouragement of her friends, and the dedication of the incredible volunteers at Rochester Playbook. Their collective efforts have resulted in a valuable resource for families, adventurers, and anyone seeking the magic of Greater Rochester's playgrounds.

ABOUT ROCHESTER'S PLAYBOOK

Rochester's Playbook is more than just a guide; it's a community-driven effort to showcase affordable family fun to the Greater Rochester Region. As a collaborative initiative, it thrives on sharing the latest updates about playgrounds and other family-friendly activities throughout the area, making it an indispensable resource for local families and visitors.

What We Do:

- Playground Insights: One of our primary focuses is to keep you informed about the latest developments in playgrounds across the Greater Rochester Region. From new builds to maintenance updates, we've got you covered.

- Family-Friendly Adventures: But we're not just about swings and slides. Rochester's Playbook is your go-to source for a wide range of family-friendly activity ideas. Whether it's a hidden gem in the city or an adventure in the scenic Finger Lakes, we've got recommendations for all.

Connect with Us:

Stay in the loop with Rochester's Playbook on Instagram and Facebook, where we regularly share updates, tips, and engaging content to enhance your family's experience in Greater Rochester. Join our community of families seeking affordable, fun-filled adventures and discover all the region has to offer. Your next exciting family outing is just a click away!

Printed in the USA
CPSIA information can be obtained
at www.ICGtesting.com
CBHW081959021223
2109CB00010B/12